The Love of Trees

October, 1975

The Love of Trees

Kenneth A. Beckett

Contents

First published 1975 by
Octopus Books Limited
59 Grosvenor Street, London W.1.

ISBN 0 7064 0425 4

Distributed in USA by
Crescent Books
a division of Crown Publishers Inc
419 Park Avenue South
New York, N.Y. 10016

Distributed in Australia by
Rigby Limited
30 North Terrace, Kent Town
Adelaide, South Australia 5067

Produced by Mandarin Publishers Limited
14 Westlands Road, Quarry Bay, Hong Kong

Printed in Hong Kong

Introduction

Trees in the landscape

Stand and face your favourite country view and try to imagine it totally devoid of trees. Unless dramatic hills or mountains are present, the result will be a dull monotony. Think also of our city parks without trees and what dismal places they would be. Even the landscape of hills or mountains is greatly embellished by trees. The undistinguished hill becomes a point of interest with a crown of beech or pine. The stark bones of the mountains are softened and beautified when clad in a tapestry of fir or spruce forest. One has to see and experience the truly desert mountains, as typified by those of the Andes of northern Chile, really to appreciate the starkness of an otherwise dramatic landscape.

In all but the driest of lands trees embellish and beautify the scene. The flatter the country the more important they are. Indeed, they are the landscape where hills are few and far between or non-existent. What splendid accent points they make, for example, as groups around the homesteads of the great plains of the USA. And how featureless would be much of the rolling landscape of eastern and midland England without its soaring hedgerow elms.

Diversity

Throughout the temperate world there are thousands of species of trees, each with a distinctive habit of growth and having leaves, flowers and fruits unique to itself. Some are evergreen, others are deciduous, losing their leaves at the onset of winter. They can be conveniently classified into two groups, the conifers or softwoods and the broadleaves or hardwoods. The first group is composed of mainly evergreen trees with an erect trunk and small lateral branches often borne in rings or whorls; firs and spruces are the most familiar examples. Most species are fast growing and have straight grained timber that is easily worked. The second group is more varied, but is largely deciduous and has a head of sturdy branches, some of which may be almost as big as the trunk. In some cases they are quick growing, in others slow growing and the wood may be tough or hard or soft; familiar examples are oak, beech, maple, chestnut, ash.

World distribution

With the exception of those regions where total aridity prevails, there are few habitats in the world that have not been exploited by trees of one sort or another. Generally speaking, the greatest number of species are found in the wetter climates and richer soils, which is hardly surprising when one considers how much food and water is required to keep an average sized tree growing healthily. The areas of the world richest in tree species are the lowland tropics, such as the Amazon and Congo river basins. Next come the temperate rain forest regions, so often in mountain ranges, of the northern hemisphere—notably western Asia, including Japan, the western and eastern USA. Smaller areas also occur in Australasia and southern South America. Most of the trees mentioned in this book come from such climates and the drier fringe areas.

Use of trees

From earliest times, trees have provided man with shelter, food and basic materials for tools and weapons, plus certain items of medicinal use. Possibly of equal importance to all these uses has been the value of wood as a fuel for fires to warm the body and cook the food. As civilization has advanced, the role of the tree in world economics and use has changed and it has now sunk to the level of a raw material fed into the maws of the paper-makers or to be torn apart chemically for the plastics industry. Happily however, town and country planners are now more aware than ever of the value of trees in the landscape. Areas of natural or semi-natural woodland are set aside as national parks or nature reserves and there is much planting for purely aesthetic purposes. A national Tree Planting Year (1973) in Britain is splendid evidence of this trend. Trees are now used as never before by planners and builders to set off the stark lines of modern buildings. Such is the hurry to create the final effect that vast and expensive machinery is now available to move large trees on to the site. An equally important role for the trees is as a screen to hide unsightly industrial buildings or as windbreaks in open exposed areas. The most splendid use of trees has been (and to a lesser extent still is) in our parks and open spaces, and on the estates of the wealthy. Here trees can be seen in small groups or singly, sited to show off their characteristic shapes, textures and colours against the smooth green background of mown grass.

Tree products

Apart from the wood, still extensively used for furniture, musical instruments, carving and other purposes already touched upon, trees yield a variety of useful products. Foremost are the various fruits such as apples, plums, cherries, peaches, apricots and figs. Man no longer relies upon picking wild tree fruits but grows selected improved forms in orchards all over the temperate world. Nuts also are important both for eating and as a source of vegetable oil. Walnut and pecan and almond are much relished by man, but acorns from the oak and beech nuts were formerly an important item for his livestock—mainly pigs. Several coniferous trees exude a sticky substance known as resin from which turpentine is extracted, while others have sap that contains sugar. The well known sugar maple (*Acer saccharum*) is the most noteworthy in this respect and in its native eastern USA and Canada quite an industry is built around collecting the sap and boiling it down for molasses. Tannin, used for processing fine leather is found in the bark of many trees, notably oak, spruce and hemlock. The bark is stripped from trees felled for timber and thus forms a useful bi-product. Many trees produce corky bark, but only one—the cork oak—yields the cork of commerce. If carefully done, the bark can be removed without killing the tree which will then grow a further layer.

Simple tree botany

Trees are woody plants. Unlike the herbaceous perennial, which grows from and dies back to ground level each year, it produces stems which become ligneous and persist, sometimes for centuries. As the stems age they thicken and become branches supported by the original stem, which becomes the trunk or bole. It is this pattern of trunk and branched head which makes the typical tree so distinctive. Difficulties of definition between trees and shrubs may arise when more than one trunk is present. In such cases, sheer size must be the criterion; anything over 15 ft in height may legitimately be called a tree.

However big a tree becomes it still functions basically in the same way as any other plant. Let us follow its life cycle from a seed. Usually as soon as the temperature starts to rise in early spring the seed coat splits and a plump white root grows down into the soil. Once the root is well anchored the stem begins to grow upwards. At this stage it is often crooked over so that the leaves it bears will be pulled gently out of the soil and not thrust upwards through it. Each seed contains two to several organs known as seed leaves (the palms have only one). In trees such as oak and chestnut the seed leaves are very fleshy and act as food reserves. Ash, birch, larch and pine, on the other hand, have thinner seed leaves which have small reserves. Oak and chestnut retain the seed leaves underground, ash and pine

larch seed
and seedling

ash seed
and seedling

bring them above ground, where they expand into green functioning leaves. Seed leaves of this origin are frequently of a different shape to the adult foliage; for example, those of the birch are very tiny and circular in outline and those of the lime are fan-shaped and deeply fingered. Quite often even the first true, or rough, leaves are not of the exact pattern as the mature tree. In the common ash, the first leaves may have only one or three leaflets, whereas later there will be seven to thirteen. The buckeye and horse chestnut have fewer leaflets and the oaks and maples fewer lobes. When the tree attains sapling size, the leaves may be larger than the final adult stage and there may be other minor characteristic differences. Because of these changes during the early years, the tree from seedling until it flowers and fruits is spoken of as juvenile.

Leaf shape among tree species varies greatly, though many seem to have variations on a theme of oval to elliptic, variously toothed and/or lobed, but sometimes smooth. Narrower leaves are lance-shaped or lanceolate, such as are borne by many willows. Even narrower leaves are linear and are typical of many conifers like pines, yews and firs. Cordate leaves have a heart-shaped base like those of the limes, while palmate leaves are typically those of the maples. The ash and the tree of heaven are good examples of a pinnate leaf—two rows of leaflets in pairs with a solitary one at the tip, though in some cases this terminal leaflet is missing. Digitate leaves are also composed of several leaflets, but here they are like the fingers of a hand, all arising at the same point, like those of the buckeye or horse chestnut.

Leaves are arranged on the tree in a characteristic pattern known as the leaf mosaic. Basically they may be in opposite pairs, spiralled or in flattened sprays—as in beech. Essentially, the mosaic ensures that each leaf gets its share of sunlight, whether direct or filtered. Just as the leaves are arranged on the twig in a certain way, so the twigs are set on the branches in a characteristic formation peculiar to each species. This in turn decides the shape of the ultimate mature tree, which can be so distinctive that the forester, gardener or botanist can tell what species it is from far off.

At first, the seeding tree or young twig is as soft as that of any annual or herbaceous perennial plant. Gradually however, the cell walls become thickened and form the tissue we know as wood. Each subsequent year a layer of these woody cells is formed outside the existing one and so builds up the branch or trunk. These layers are known as annual rings. The woody cells which comprise each annual ring are tubular, and transport water and dissolved mineral salts up to the leaves. In spring the cells are large in order to take the increased flow of essential water. Later in the year growth slows down and they are smaller. Thus the rings are demarked by layers of small and

Leaf shapes

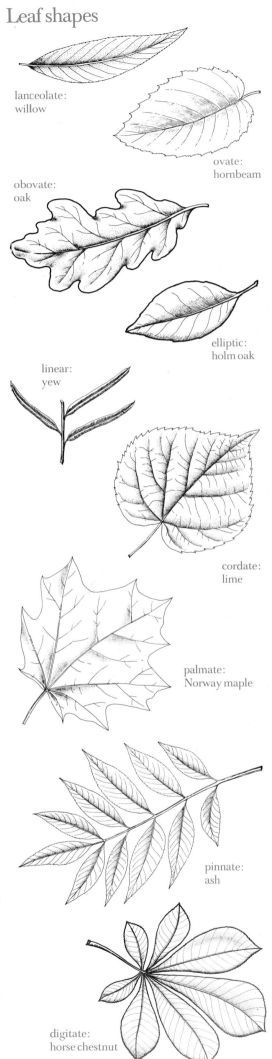

lanceolate:
willow

ovate:
hornbeam

obovate:
oak

elliptic:
holm oak

linear:
yew

cordate:
lime

palmate:
Norway maple

pinnate:
ash

digitate:
horse chestnut

large tubular cells and readily counted, making it easy to tell the age of a particular log or cut branch. During the good years when rainfall and sunshine averages are high, an annual ring may be much wider than average and during a poor year, or after some shock, as when it is lifted and transplanted, much smaller. The tree might be seared with fire or damaged by lightning and after the wound has covered over with healing callous tissue the depositing of annual rings continues. A trunk or large branch of a tree can therefore be used as a sort of calendar and the study of tree rings has now become a respectable branch of the natural sciences under the name of dendrochronology.

Both soft green stems and in particular the leaves carry out a process known as photosynthesis. This takes place between the green colouring matter chlorophyll, carbon dioxide and water by the action of the energy provided by the sun's rays. The products of photosynthesis are carbon compounds, notably sugars, which later are turned to starches. As a bi-product, oxygen is given off. Scientists have computed that most, if not all, of the world's oxygen supply originated from plant life in this way. The carbon compounds in conjunction with the dissolved mineral salts in the water supply from the roots provide all the basic ingredients for growth, plus several substances, apparently in the nature of bi-products, such as rubber latex and resins, which are of great use to man.

One of the most fascinating and as yet unsolved riddles of tree structure is how the sap, taken from the soil via the roots, travels to the top of a tall tree. It is known that leaves are continuously giving off water vapour which creates a pull on the stream of water from below, but this is hardly enough to get it to the top of a 350 ft tall sequoia (redwood) or eucalyptus. Several theories have been put forward but so far none are as yet fully proven.

The juvenile phase of a tree's life passes with its first flowering. This may be less than ten years for such quick growing trees as sycamore, maple and some poplars to as long as forty years for some of the oaks. All trees produce flowers eventually, though they may be small or dull coloured and insignificant. Flowers, whether of trees or any other kind of plant which bears them, are composed of modified leaves. They contain the sexual organs of the plant known as the pistil (female) and stamens (male). When young and immature they are protected by leaf-like organs known as petals and sepals, though in some trees these may be missing, the protective wrapping being supplied by further modified leaves known as bracts—the catkins of alder, willow and poplar being examples. In such trees as magnolia, the petals are large and coloured and act also as an attraction for insects that pollinate them. Stamens are composed of a stalk and two anther lobes or pollen sacs. The pollen contained is the male element and the

equivalent of sperm in the animal kingdom. Each pistil is made up of the ovary—which later becomes the fruit—and a stigma joined to the ovary by a stalk known as a style. The stigma is either sticky or bears hairs which trap the pollen grains. Pollen can be transported by insects or wind, the latter means being common among trees. Such pollen, as for example that of the pines or poplars, bears minute air bladders which enables it to ride even light winds. On reaching the stigma it germinates, each grain sending out a pollen tube into the ovary where its nucleus fuses with the nearest ovule. This fusion results in the formation of a seed, usually contained within a fruit which develops from the ovary. It must here be noted that in a botanical sense, a fruit is a ripened ovary and can be hard and dry, like a nut or fleshy as in cherry, plum and apple.

If all the seeds a tree produces were to fall to the ground immediately beneath, the resulting seedlings would soon be starved of food and light and never have a chance of developing into an adult tree. During the evolutionary history of the many and varied tree species their fruits or seeds have developed means of dispersal which effectively removes them from the parent and often sends them far and wide to colonize new territory. Not all tree fruits or seeds appear to be specially modified for dispersal. Acorns from the oak and the nuts from the buckeye and chestnut often fall straight to the ground below. However, these seeds are smooth and rounded and may bounce or roll on hitting the ground, particularly if it slopes. Most years there will be at least one period of high winds as the seeds ripen and as the branches and twigs are flung back and forth the seeds can be catapulted surprisingly long distances. Acorns and similar nut-like seeds are also sometimes carried off by birds such as crows and as they are hard and smooth may easily slip from the bill and fall far from the parent tree. The common oak is spread by this means.

Many tree seeds have appendages adapted to dispersal by wind. Maple and ash fruits have broad, horny wings, while the seeds of birch and pine have delicate membranous ones. The tiny seeds of willow and poplar are embedded in a tuft of cottonwool-like hairs and are often carried many miles by strong winds. In some cases, the fruit or a cluster of fruits remain attached to a persistent leaf-like bract, which acts like a wing when the whole cluster is whisked from the twig by autumn gales. The various kinds of lime and hornbeam are examples of this mode of travel. Several trees have buoyant, woody fruits which float on water and can be dispersed by rivers and the sea. Most of the examples are tropical in origin, the coconut being the best known. Among temperate trees, the bean-like seeds of *Sophora tetraptera* or the kowai, the national flower of New Zealand, can float in sea-water for several months and have drifted across the

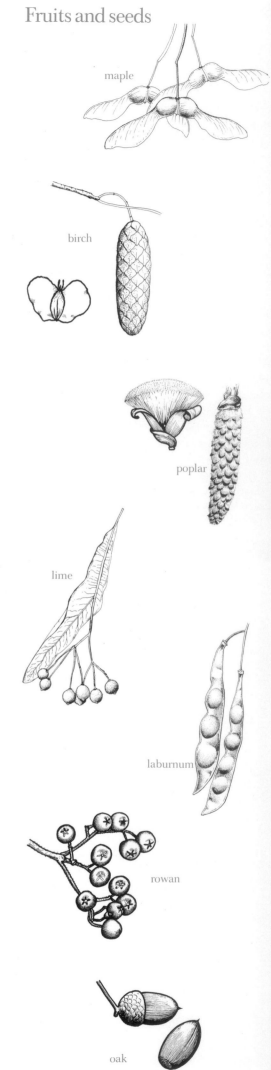

Fruits and seeds

maple

birch

poplar

lime

laburnum

rowan

oak

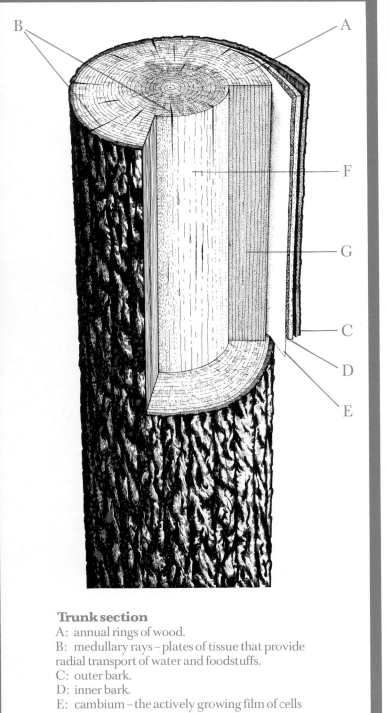

Trunk section
A: annual rings of wood.
B: medullary rays – plates of tissue that provide radial transport of water and foodstuffs.
C: outer bark.
D: inner bark.
E: cambium – the actively growing film of cells that produces the annual rings of wood.
F: dead heart wood.
G: living sap wood through which water passes up to the leaves.

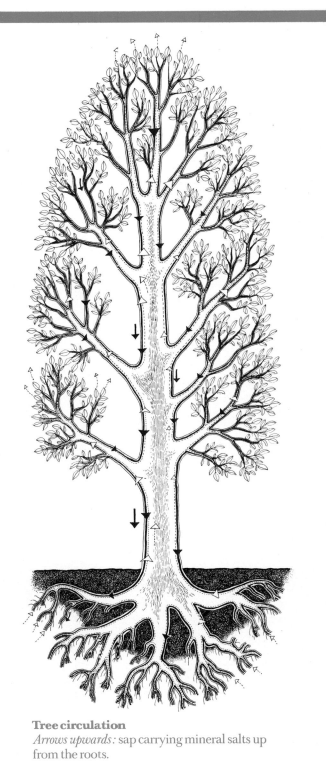

Tree circulation
Arrows upwards: sap carrying mineral salts up from the roots.
Arrows downwards: return sap flow carrying sugars elaborated in the leaves.

Pacific to give rise to the Chilean population of this attractive, yellow, pea-flowered species.

Many plants have dry fruits which split suddenly and expel the seeds well away from the parent, but this method of dispersal is rare among temperate trees. Laburnum or golden rain has pods which split open, but very few of the seeds are actually expelled. Later the dried halves of the pod with some seeds still attached may be detached by strong winds and blown away to a new site. Also rare among the trees are fruits with barbs or hooks which cling to the fur or feathers of animals or birds and are thus dispersed. Fleshy fruits such as apples, cherries, plums, rowan berries and many others, provide the animals and birds which

disperse the seeds with a meal as a reward. The actual seeds—cherry and plum stones or apple pips—have a very hard and horny coat able to resist the digestive juices of the animal. Later they pass out of the animal or bird in its droppings and germinate all the more readily when compared with those which have not had such an experience. Birds are the main agents in this method of dispersal and can travel several miles between the eating of the fruits and voiding of the seeds. Having been successfully dispersed to a favourable new site, the seed finally germinates and the whole cycle is complete.

The selection of trees that follows is essentially a personal one, and while it sets out to present a comprehensive cross-section of the numerous species of temperate trees, it cannot, however, hope to be exhaustive. The groupings in general are a matter of convenience and do not follow a botanical classification. They work by associating essential characteristics or uses, or the linkages in the popular mind, such as ash, beech, oak; juniper and yew; edible fruits; trees with pods. The essential thing is that the wonder and beauty of trees is brought into the home and that as a result they will be looked at with new eyes and appreciation in our ever eroded countryside.

Redwood, Cypress, Arbor vitae

There are few tree spectacles more dramatic than the first sight of a grove of redwoods or the Brobdignagian bole of the aptly named big tree, soaring upwards among lesser brethren. The redwood or coast redwood (*Sequoia sempervirens*) and the big tree (*Sequoiadendron giganteum*) are evergreen conifers of ancient lineage, and closely related species have been found fossilized in the rocks of several countries.

Nowadays they are restricted to the states of California and adjacent Oregon. The big tree grows in the high valleys of the Sierra Nevada in California, where it occurs as small groups and scattered individuals among pines, incense cedars and other trees. Large specimens are of immense and unbelievable size. One of the largest, named General Sherman, is over 100 ft in circumference at the base. Larger specimens have existed. The stump of one of these was used as a dance floor and could easily take thirty-two couples. The cypress-like foliage of the big tree is small and scaly, arranged in stiff, plumy branchlets. Considering the size of the tree, the cones and seeds are surprisingly small. Ovoid and hard, each cone ranges from $1\frac{1}{2}-2\frac{1}{2}$ in long. Contained within are several, small, winged seeds, the actual living part no bigger than a match head—small beginnings indeed for the world's largest tree!

Although the largest in sheer bulk, the big tree is exceeded in height by the coast redwood. This more slender tree has flattened needle-like leaves up to 1 in long and more rounded, smaller cones. It is native to the fog belt of California and just into Oregon and often grows in dense communities. Walking among the enormous, red-brown, fluted columns makes one feel like an ant in a corn field! Many specimens exceed 300 ft and at least one tree was 367 ft tall when measured a few years ago. Both the redwood and the big tree are typified by possessing enormously thick, spongy bark with an almost asbestos quality. This protects the trunks from the many forest fires that can rage so devastatingly through their respective homelands.

The cypresses can be grouped into two sections; the true cypresses (*Cupressus*) with small scale leaves arranged in plume-like branchlets, and the so-called false cypresses (*Chamaecyparis*) with often smaller leaves arranged in flat sprays. All are evergreen and many make fine specimen trees for the garden.

Much planted in Great Britain, New Zealand, Australia and other mild temperate areas is the Monterey cypress (*Cupressus macrocarpa*). Surprisingly enough, this vigorous tree is on the verge of extinction in its native home. A few small groves and scattered groups only exist on the wild and rugged California coast around Monterey. They are carefully protected, but seem to produce few self-sown seedlings. In the wild the tree is broad-headed, often branched right from the ground. Many specimens are wind-swept into bizarre shapes and fit in beautifully with the rock strewn landscape. In gardens it forms at first a pyramidal tree, broadening out with age.

Left: *Sequoia sempervirens*
Right: *Sequoiadendron giganteum*
Below: *Cupressus macrocarpa*

Large specimens can attain 70 ft or more. Smaller growing and rather more decorative with its smoky grey or blue-green foliage is the smooth Arizona cypress (*C. glabra*). It comes from the mountains of central Arizona where it was first discovered as recently as 1907. It is confused in gardens with the similar *C. arizonica* from the states of Arizona, New Mexico and adjacent Mexico. It may be easily distinguished from *C. glabra* by its reddish bark, rough on the trunk and smooth on the branches.

All who have had the luck to visit the countries bordering the northern shores of the Mediterranean, particularly those along the eastern half, are impressed by the pencil slim outlines of the Italian or Mediterranean cypress (*C. sempervirens*). A group of these dark green columns stalking across a rocky, sun-soaked landscape, perhaps framed by a sparkling, deep blue sea, create that essential Mediterranean atmosphere. This very narrow, columnar tree is in fact an erect form unknown in the wild. It appears to have arisen as a sport or mutant from a more spreading branched, wild species which can often be seen mixed with the narrow ones. Where these trees seed themselves on the hillsides one can usually find every grade, from pencil to quite broad cone shapes.

To see the most magnificent of the false cypresses one must journey again to the USA and adjacent Canada. Here, in the moist climate of south-west Oregon and north-west California may be seen the Port Orford Cedar or Lawson Cypress—to mention its two commonest vernacular names—(*Chamaecyparis lawsoniana*). Here, great columns of frond-like, grey-green foliage soar up to 150 and occasionally 200 ft. When young, it forms narrowly conical specimens of great decorative value, and it is much planted in the gardens of the temperate world, providing the climate is not too dry and hot. Many different mutant forms have arisen, some of them in shades of grey, blue-green, yellow and gold.

Heading north to the strip of country that

starts at the Cascade Mountains of northern Oregon and ends in Alaska at Prince William Sound, one can see the Nootka cypress (*C. nootkatensis*). A little less tall and more spreading than the Lawson cypress, this tree is very much more elegant, especially when young, when its vertically pendulous, fern-frondlike branchlets can be seen to advantage. Globular cones, spiked all over like an old-fashioned sea mine, add a touch of fascination.

Far left: *Cupressus sempervirens* (erect and spreading-branched forms)
Left: *Chamaecyparis nootkatensis*
Above right: Cones and foliage of *Chamaecyparis lawsoniana*
Below right: Cones and foliage of *Chamaecyparis nootkatensis*

From Japan comes the Hinoki cypress (*C. obtusa*) having the small scale leaves thickened towards the blunt tip and bearing waxy, white markings. In the wilds of its central and southern Japanese home it can attain 100 ft or more in height and is much valued as a timber tree. The wood is light, strong, durable and gives a glossy finish. It is much in demand for high-class building construction particularly houses, bridges and furniture. The Sawara cypress (*C. pisifera*) has a similar distribution in Japan and has given rise to many decorative forms much grown in the gardens of the temperate world. Several of these forms have slender curved and pointed juvenile leaves which create a plumy effect *en masse*.

False and true cypresses have come together to give us a most decorative and fast growing tree known as the Leyland cypress (*X Cupressocyparis leylandii*). In 1888 at Leighton Hall, Welshpool, Wales, seeds from *Chamaecyparis nootkatensis* were sown. Near to the parent tree was a specimen of *Cupressus macrocarpa* and when the seedlings were well grown six were seen to be of hybrid origin. It was some years, however, before the trees excited any interest and the hybrid was only described for the first time by W. Dallimore in 1925. Seedlings have also been raised with *Cupressus macrocarpa* as the female parent. The Leyland cypress forms a broadly columnar tree not unlike the Nootka cypress, but less pendulous. When well sited its speed of growth is phenomenal; 30 year old specimens can, on average, be expected to exceed 60 ft.

Much resembling the false cypresses and having similar scale leaves and frondlike growth are the various sorts of arbor vitae (*Thuja*). Ranging in size from a rounded bush to a small dense tree 30 ft or more tall is the Chinese arbor vitae (*T. orientalis*). It is easily identified by the distinctive way in which the flattened branchlets are held vertically side by side like the pages of a book. Equally diagnostic are the little, freely borne cones, each scale of which has a curved spike sometimes bent enough to suggest a shepherd's crook. Rejoicing in such names as eastern arbor vitae, white cedar and northern white cedar, *T. occidentalis* is a larger tree achieving 50–60 ft in its native eastern North America. The trunk is often quite massive and buttressed and the branches are held horizontally. When bruised, the foliage gives off a pleasant aromatic small.

The aristocrat of the genus is undoubtedly the western red cedar (*T. plicata*). Still sometimes listed under its older name of *T. lobbii*, this tree rivals the Lawson cypress in height, sometimes attaining 200 ft. The growth is a lighter green than Lawson and has a delightfully sweet and aromatic smell when bruised. It is native to the north-western area of North America, including part of Alaska, where it is an important timber tree. Growing as a solitary specimen and with its cinnamon brown trunk this is a majestic tree both in the wild and cultivation.

Although related to the giant big tree and coast redwood, the swamp cypress or bald cypress (*Taxodium distichum*) is a very different tree in appearance. 'Bald' is a good name for this deciduous species which stands bald of leaves all winter. It forms a rounded tipped, cone-shaped outline well filled with slender branchlets and stems. These erupt into a mist of bright green, needle-like foliage in spring and rival the larch in appeal. In autumn the same leaves turn russet brown and fall with the small twigs that bear them. Although originally found in swamps in its native south-eastern USA it also thrives in ordinary, moisture retentive garden soils. When growing by or actually in water this tree produces unique structures from its roots known as knees. These are erect, cylindrical protuberances, usually rather knobbly and stand above ground or water. It is thought that they provide an air supply for the submerged roots.

The bald or swamp cypress is little planted nowadays, its place having been taken by the equally, if not more, decorative dawn redwood (*Metasequoia glyptostroboides*). Surprisingly enough, this Chinese species was only discovered in 1941 in Szechwan by T. Kan, of Nanking University. In 1946 an expedition went to the area and collected seeds, some of which were distributed in North America, Europe and eastern Asia. Trees raised from this seed have grown well in a variety of climates, forming slender pyramids which are highly decorative when covered with larch green leaves in spring. It thrives best in a moist soil.

Above: *Thuya plicata*
Right: *Taxodium distichum*

Spruce, Fir, Hemlock

Famed in Europe as the Christmas tree, the Norway spruce or common spruce (*Picea abies*) forms an elegant tree that can achieve 200 ft in height under ideal conditions. It typifies all the spruce and fir species in having a straight, mast-like stem or trunk with the comparatively small branches carried in rings or whorls along its length. The Norway spruce has lower branches that sweep downwards with a flourish, whilst the upper ones stand out horizontally. The rich green, needle-like leaves are borne densely along the twigs, each one attached to a short, peg-like projection. This clearly distinguishes it and other spruces from the true firs (*Abies* species) which have the leaves attached to the twigs by round, sucker-like stalks. Mature trees bear pendulous, glossy brown cones on the upper branches rather like fat, scaly cigars. They release small, oval nutlets attached to a membranous wing, which ride the winds and travel far and wide.

Also European is the Serbian or Servian spruce (*P. omorika*) which graces the mountains of Yugoslavia. Rather similar to *P. abies*, it is even more elegant in appearance, forming a very slender spire up to 100 ft tall.

Although the Engelmann spruce (*P. engelmannii*) is a rather variable species in its most shapely form it may be looked upon as a western American version of the Serbian spruce. It has a tremendous range in the wild, frequenting the mountains of New Mexico north to British Columbia and Alaska.

Thriving under similar conditions is the blue spruce or Colorado spruce (*P. pungens*). The prickle-pointed needles of this tree may be green but are more likely to be an intense blue-white with a smoky quality to its overall colour. To come upon a grove or group of Colorado spruce, whether in its mountain homeland or in a park or arboretum, is a sight to behold, for the intensity of colour is unreal —like thick blue frost.

Considered by many to be the most beautiful of all the fifty known spruces is Brewer's weeping spruce (*Picea breweriana*). This rare tree was discovered in the Siskiyou Mountains by Professor Brewer in 1863, but it was not until twenty years later that it was named by

Far left: *Picea abies*
Top: *Picea engelmannii*
Left: *Picea omorika*
Above: *Picea breweriana*

the Oregon botanist, T. Howell, in honour of the discoverer. It is found only in a few localities in the wild in a strip of mountainous country straddling the western Oregon/California boundary. A well developed specimen, at least up to middle age, is broadly conical in outline, well furnished with whorls of branches that sweep outwards like a lightly strung longbow. From each of these branches frond-like branchlets depend vertically one behind the other like an elegant, rich green drapery.

Apart from the leaf character that distinguishes the spruces from the firs (already mentioned on page 16) the other clear and obvious point of separation is the erect, long, oval cones, which sit like candles along the upper branches of mature trees. When ripe, these slowly disintegrate to release the winged seeds to the mercy of wind and gale. When young and soft, these cones are highly attractive with hues of slate-blue and violet, often with a waxy white patina. Most species of fir however produce them too high up to be admired and appreciated. An exception to this is the Korean fir (*Abies koreana*) which produces its violet cones when still very small, sometimes when less than 3 ft tall. Eventually it can reach 30 ft or more but takes many years to do so. The needles are a rich, bright green above and white beneath, a striking contrast. In the wild it is found only on Quelpaert, an island off the coast of Korea and where it was first discovered in 1907.

On Mount Enos in Cephalonia there is a vast grove of the Grecian fir (*A. cephalonica*). The grove was formerly almost fifteen miles long but has been greatly decimated by forest fires. The Grecian fir also occurs on several other of Greece's higher mountains, clothing the rocky slopes with their glistening green, rather curved, needles. Well grown specimens can attain 100 ft in height. The 6 in long cones are intriguing objects, being composed of brown, fan-shaped scales, from which protrude narrow bracts with triangular points, just like tiny dragons' tongues.

The 2–3 in long needles of white fir or Colorado white fir (*Abies concolor*) are distinc-

tively arranged on each side of the shoot like the teeth of a comb. They are usually a pleasing shade of grey or blue-green. In the mountains of its south-western USA homeland this species can be of massive dimensions reaching sometimes 200 ft and with a trunk diameter up to 5 ft. Such a bole, clad in deeply fissured ashen grey bark, perhaps 6 in thick, is an impressive sight.

From the Olympic and Cascade Mountains and adjacent areas of Oregon and Washington states comes the aptly named noble fir (*A. nobilis*). Regrettably, botanists have now changed the name of this truly noble tree to *A. procera*, which means tall, but otherwise gives no indication of its appearance. First

discovered by that intrepid, lone plant collector, David Douglas, on the south side of the Columbia River in 1825, this tree can attain a total height of 150 ft and a girth of 24 ft. The somewhat curved needles have a blue-white hue, which lends a smoky effect to the great columns of foliage when viewed from a distance. Having a wide distribution on the North American continent and extending well north into Canada, the balsam fir (*A. balsamea*) is better known to Europeans as a source of Canada balsam. This resinous substance is obtained from bark blisters and is used in varnishes and for other purposes. Its wood is much used for paper making.

Left: *Abies cephalonica*
Above: *Abies procera*

Closely related to *Abies* and at one time classified in that genus, are the seven known species of Douglas fir (*Pseudotsuga*). The best known of these is the original Douglas fir (*P. menziesii*) which was originally discovered by Archibald Menzies, a Scottish naval surgeon and botanist who accompanied the explorer Captain George Vancouver during his epic four year voyage charting the northern Pacific (1791–5). The Douglas fir has an extensive distribution in the western USA and Canada, with outlying colonies as far east as the Grand Canyon in Arizona. Under ideal conditions it can reach 300 ft in height and almost rivals the redwoods, while retaining a remarkably slim and elegant outline. Large specimens develop a deeply fissured bark that may become 12 in thick. The oval brown cones are pendulous from the twigs and have forked tongue-like bracts protruding from the scales.

Hemlock spruce or hemlock is the vernacular name for a widespread genus of handsome conifers which rather resemble the spruces in habit of growth. The leaves are much shorter and broader, however, and arranged in flattened rows on either side of the twigs. The eastern hemlock (*Tsuga canadensis*) is somewhat irregularly, broadly pyramidal in habit with elegantly downswept branches, that can become spangled with tiny acorn-shaped cones. The leaves are dark green above and have blue-white bands beneath.

The western hemlock (*T. heterophylla*) is more neatly pyramidal or spire-like in outline and can reach a much greater height—250ft and more having been recorded.

Above: *Tsuga heterophylla*
Right: *Pseudotsugo menziesii*

Pine, Larch, Cedar

Imagine a pine cone like a large pineapple, each scale of which is armed with a stout, incurved woody spike; a large one could be 14 in long and weigh 4–5 lb. Such a cone is not imaginary and is borne by Coulter's pine (*Pinus coulteri*) a native of dry mountain slopes in California. It forms a stout branched pyramidal tree, clad with slender needles, that range from 6–12 in long and are borne in groups of three. Of all the 100 different species of pine, Coulter's has the largest (but not the longest) and heaviest cones. Only one other species in any way rivals it, this being the digger pine (*P. sabiniana*), also from California and named after the Digger Indians who relished the nutty, sepia brown, edible seeds. The award for the longest pine cone must go to the sugar pine (*P. lambertiana*), yet another native of California and one which also holds the record as the tallest pine. Extending northwards into Oregon, this tree is one of the most prominent members of the Sierra Nevada timber belt. Under ideal conditions it can attain 250 ft, much of this being a vast, column-like bole supporting a most charac-teristic head of horizontal and ascending branches with a rather sparse leafage. From the branch tips depend enormous banana-shaped cones which vary from 12–18 in long. They are composed of broad, thin, pale-brown, tipped scales and for their size are very light. Spirally twisted, firm and pointed, the 3–4 in long needles are borne in clusters of five.

This pine is so called, owing to the sugary resin that is exuded mainly from charred or wounded trunks. It is another of David Douglas's finds and he records that the ripe cones were so far above his head that the only way was to shoot them off with his rifle; luckily he was a very good shot!

Related to the Lambert pine is the Mexican white pine (*P. ayacahuite*), but the slender grey-green leaves, also in groups of five are spreading and can be up to 8 in long. The cones range from 9–15 in long and larger ones have been recorded. Although a decorative species and useful as a specimen tree or windbreak, the white pine (*P. strobus*) is more important as a timber tree in its native, eastern USA and Canada. It has several vernacular names notably yellow pine, apple pine, pumpkin pine, New England pine and northern pine; in Britain it is known as the Weymouth pine after Lord Weymouth who planted it widely at his Longleat estate in Wiltshire. It is another pine with its needles in fives and has a similar but smaller cone to that of the two previously mentioned species.

One of the most ornamental of all pines is the rough-branched Mexican pine (*P. mon-tezumae*) another of the five-leaved group. It can achieve 80 ft or more in its native Central American mountain homeland and has intense blue-grey, drooping needles, which on a dull day seem to shine with a radiance of their own.

Dull by comparison, but not lacking in a certain rugged charm is the European black or Austrian pine (*P. nigra*). This has dark green needles borne in pairs and 2–3 in long cones of tawny-yellow aging to brown. It is a splendid tree for a windbreak and will succeed on thin poor soils of limestone or sand.

Left: *Pinus montezumae*
Right: *Pinus nigra*

The same can be said of the Scots pine (*P. sylvestris*), but this widespread native of Europe and western Asia is a more picturesque tree with a straight, reddish trunk and a rather rounded head when mature. A windswept group on a moorland skyline adds just that right touch and makes the scene without monopolizing it. The grey-green needles are borne in pairs and vary from 1–4 in in length. In Europe and particularly Britain, this pine is much used for re-afforestation. The wood is of excellent quality and easily worked and is used for a wide variety of purposes under the names of whitewood, yellow deal, red deal and Norway fir.

Of all the pines, none is planted in such a worldwide fashion as the Monterey pine (*P. radiata*). In Australia, New Zealand and South Africa thousands of acres of this fast-growing tree have been planted, mainly to provide timber for building construction and box making. Under ideal conditions as much as 6 ft of growth can be made in one year. It is a handsome species with rather dense, glossy bright-green needles borne in threes and is native to the coast of California.

The western yellow pine (*P. ponderosa*) has a wide distribution in the western half of the USA. It is a tall and majestic species reaching 150 ft and occasionally 180 ft with a bole diameter of up to 6 ft. The 5–10 in long leaves are borne in threes and are a rich yellow-green, a shade and texture which picks up the low-angle rising and setting sun and seems to illuminate the tree from within. At maturity the 3–6 in long cones are a deep plum-purple and contrast strikingly with the foliage.

Departing from the norm of pine form, the stone pine (*P. pinea*) develops a dense rounded head of picturesque appearance and is a characteristic sight in its Mediterranean homeland. Umbrella pine is an alternative vernacular name and as the tree matures and widens in the crown it does almost take on an umbrella outline. The 4–6 in long, dark green needles are borne in pairs and are slightly twisted. Almost globose in shape, the 5–6 in long cones can carry as many as one hundred

seeds. These are thick shelled and nut-like and contain a pleasantly edible kernel.

The umbrella pine is not related to the true pines and in fact belongs to the same family as the redwood and swamp cypress. However it rather resembles a pine and has the same sort of appeal. Botanically known as *Sciadopitys verticillata*, this tree is a native of Honshu, Japan where it grows on steep, rocky mountainsides. It bears leaves of two kinds—tiny triangular ones that soon become red-brown and membranous, and slender needle-like leaves which can attain 5 in in length. These latter appear anatomically to be two leaves fused together and are arranged in whorls of ten to thirty. They are a rich, dark green and clothe the slender spire-like tree to perfection.

Left: *Pinus sylvestris*
Below: *Pinus radiata*

The various kinds of larch (*Larix*) are botanically related to the true pines but do not closely resemble them in any way. All twelve species are deciduous, pyramidal trees with small, very slender leaves, some of which are borne in rings or whorls, like those of the umbrella pine, others scattered along the leading shoots. In spring they become beautifully garbed in young leaves of the most exquisite, tender bright green. Mature trees are, at the same time, spangled with pink or red 'flowers' (really immature cones waiting to be pollinated). In autumn, most of the species turn to shades of amber or yellow and then russet as the leaves fall.

The common larch (*Larix decidua*) comes from the Alps and Carpathians and is widely planted elsewhere for its durable timber. Well grown specimens can attain 150 ft or more in height. The Japanese larch (*L. kaempferi*, formerly *L. leptolepis*) is rather similar but can easily be distinguished by its waxy red twigs, resinous buds and globose cones (those of *decidua* are ovoid). Of particular interest is the hybrid between them known as the Dunkeld larch (*L.x eurolepis*) which arose spontaneously at Dunkeld, Perthshire, Scotland, where the

Far left: *Pinus ponderosa*
Above: *Pinus pinea*
Left: Foliage of *Sciadopitys verticillata*

parent species were planted together. This is a
very vigorous hybrid, soon outstripping both
parents in the height race. A tree planted in
1904 (or later) was 101 ft tall fifty-four years
later. The tamarack or American larch (*L.
laricina*) is rather like a smaller version of the
common larch but with cones only half the
size ($\frac{1}{2}-\frac{3}{4}$ in long). It is tolerant of both wet and
dry soils and grows rather slowly outside its
native land.

In the eyes of many tree lovers, the golden
larch (*Pseudolarix amabilis*) is the most beautiful
of all. It is distinguished from the true larch by
its larger-scaled cones, which resemble small
globe artichokes, and fall apart when ripe. In
its native China it is known as 'chin-lo-sung',
which translates to golden deciduous pine,
referring to the rich gold of its autumn foliage.

The way the leaves are borne in the larches
is the same for the true cedar (*Cedrus*), but
there the resemblance ends. Cedars are
evergreen and bear large, ovoid cones erect
on the branches. When young, all four species
of *Cedrus* form elegant spires. As they mature,
the upper branches form a broad, often flat-
topped head with the horizontal branches in
layers.

The cedar of Lebanon (*C. libani*) has biblical
associations and was once fairly abundant in
the mountains of Lebanon, but alas no more,
being now restricted to a few small groves. It is,
however, still common in the Cilician Taurus.
Much planted around mansions and chateaux
of Europe and particularly Britain, it forms a
nobly picturesque specimen tree when gracing
a spacious lawn, adding a majesty and
serenity to the scene.

The Atlas cedar (*C. atlantica*) is rather
similar, but with the leaves of blue-grey. The
deodar (*C. deodara*) is the giant of the group, in
its Himalayan homeland reaching 200 ft. It is
less massive than the previously mentioned
species, has slightly longer leaves and
drooping tips to the branchlets and leader.

Apart from its vernacular name of Japanese
cedar, *Cryptomeria japonica* has no close botanical link with the true cedars. Like the Japanese
umbrella pine, it is a 'one-off' genus and
belongs to the same family as the redwood. Its
closest resemblances are also to the redwood,
though it is a much smaller tree, rarely
exceeding 150 ft. The pointed leaves are
flattened vertically and winged at the base,
merging imperceptibly into the stem. They
adorn the spreading and drooping branches in
a lush and satisfying way. Probably the most
impressive feature of this tree is its smooth,
shaftlike bole, clad in reddish bark. Such
beautiful living columns grace many of the
Japanese shrines and give their environs shade
and serenity.

Like the Japanese cedar, the incense cedar
is only a cedar by name, its botanical affinities
placing it beside the cypresses and arbor-
vitae. Formerly known as, and often still
referred to as *Libocedrus* by gardeners, the
incense cedar is now correctly *Calocedrus*

decurrens. A native of the Sierra Nevada in California and Oregon, it forms a graceful broad pyramid of flattened branchlets composed of tiny, scale leaves. Winged seeds are contained within narrowly ovoid cones $\frac{3}{4}$ in long, which are made up of a few, very narrow scales.

Top left: *Pinus strobus*
Bottom left: *Cedrus libani*
Top right: *Larix decidua*
Bottom right: *Cedrus atlantica*

Juniper, Yew and Allies

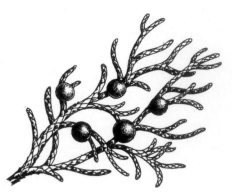

All the coniferous trees mentioned in this section are distinct in bearing fruits that look much more like berries than cones. Botanically, however, they are modified cones with from one to a few fleshy scales. Most distinctive are the various sorts of yew, which bear mucilaginous red fruits like small cups, each with a polished nutlet in the bottom. The fleshy cup is edible, but insipid, the seed and leaves poisonous.

The common yew (*Taxus baccata*), is a round-headed tree, with a reddish trunk often so deeply fissured to appear as if compounded of several smaller boles. Frequently, leafy shoots surround it. The leaves are very narrow, pointed and dark green and an excellent foil

for the red fruits. In early spring the tiny, rounded, male catkins shed vast clouds of pale yellow pollen with every gust of wind, sometimes covering the earth and vegetation for yards around with a film of the fine, bright dust. The timber is hard and very durable, which has given rise to the old saying 'a post of yew outlives a post of iron'. Two of the oldest known wooden weapons, palaeolithic spears found in Britain and Germany, are made from this wood.

Very similar is the Japanese yew (*T. cuspidata*), though it is often only of large shrub stature in European gardens. In its native mountain woods of Honshu and Hokkaido it forms a neat, round-headed tree and bears

dark green, narrowly oblong leaves that taper abruptly to a small, spiny tip.

Known by its Maori name of 'rimu' and also as red pine (*Dacrydium cupressinum*) is an important and very decorative timber tree in New Zealand. During its early years it forms a slender pyramid with weeping branchlets clad in bright green awl-shaped leaves. As it ages it becomes less shapely and the foliage changes to the adult form of smaller and thicker, almost scale-like leaves. The fruits are intriguing, resembling those of yew turned inside out, the small, ovoid nutlet sitting on the top of a fleshy red 'berry'.

Podocarp is the abbreviated and vernacular form of the botanical generic name *Podocarpus*

bestowed by foresters upon the 100 known species of mainly tropical and southern hemisphere trees. They are allied to *Dacrydium*, but bear their seeds within an oval, often fleshy, plum-like fruit. Several species are important timber trees in their respective native lands, such as the New Zealand *P. ferrugineus*, often known by its Maori name 'miro'. It forms a rather yew-like tree up to 80 ft or so and is particularly attractive when hung with small fruits just like pale crimson plums. Hardiest of the podocarps that form trees (several alpine species are of shrub stature only) is *P. macrophyllus*, in Japan called 'inu-maki'. Native also to China, it forms a small tree with stout branches and bright green narrow leaves that can attain 5 in in length and taper to a slender point.

Rather similar is the Chilean manio (*P. salignus*), but the leaves are a little shorter and narrower and the branchlets tend to droop.

Also bearing plum-like fruits are the various kinds of *Torreya*, named after Dr. John Torrey (1796–1873) one of the most famous American botanists in his day and who described many American plants for the first time. Perhaps best known of all is the California nutmeg (*T. californica*), a 90 ft tree when well grown, sometimes with a trunk girth of 9 ft. Both the the wood and broad needle-like leaves are aromatic. The Japanese nutmeg tree (*T.*

nucifera) is equally massive and with an even greater bole size, some specimens attaining a girth of 15 ft. Smaller, rigid leaves have a pungent odour when bruised. It is sometimes cultivated in the milder parts of Europe and the USA, but rarely attains even small tree size there.

Most of the junipers are shrubs, but a few achieve small to medium tree size and one at least forms a timber tree up to 100 ft. The latter is the pencil cedar (*Juniperus virginiana*) which in the wild has a wide distribution in eastern North America from Texas north to Quebec. It forms a slender pyramid of tiny grey-green, scale-like foliage among which are borne rounded to oval, greenish, berry-like

cones. Like many coniferous trees, seedlings and young trees produce leaves different from those on adult specimens. In this case, the narrow, pointed, awl-shaped juvenile foliage often appears mixed with true adult foliage on quite old trees. The soft, rather brittle, pinkish wood is surprisingly durable and is often used for making pencils. A fragrant oil is distilled from the wood shavings and used to scent soap and in perfumery.

Opposite page left: *Taxus baccata* 'Fastigiata'
Opposite page right: Fruit and foliage of *Taxus baccata*
Centre above: Fruit and foliage of *Dacrydium cupressinum*
Centre below: Fruit and foliage of *Podocarpus ferrugineus*
Right: Foliage of *Podocarpus salignus*

Kauri, Monkey puzzle, Maidenhair

The first settlers in New Zealand were astonished at the vast size of trees the Maoris called 'kauri' (*Agathis australis*) and with just reason. Even those who have first seen the redwoods and big trees of California are usually impressed by the smooth, pale grey boles that soar up perhaps for 80 ft without a branch, their heads well out of sight above the other trees of the forest. Really big specimens are now restricted in number and some of the most famous specimens have Maori names. A fine example is 'Tane Mahuta' in the Waipoua Forest on the eastern side of the toe of North Island. The last time this tree was measured it was 168 ft tall and with a girth at chest height of 45 ft 2 in. The trunk barely tapers up to the first branch and is a majestic sight indeed. Kauri, or kauri pine as it is sometimes called, though it is not related to the true pines, has a rather disappointing head, the branches being rather gaunt and open, with sparse foliage. This refers to mature specimens, young ones are neatly pyramidal in outline and remind one of their near allies the monkey puzzle and Norfolk Island pine. The striking smoothness of even the oldest kauri boles is maintained by the continuous shedding of small flakes of bark. These fall to the ground around the base and are turned into humus as good as the finest leaf mould of temperate deciduous woodlands. Over the years this builds up into a sizeable mound laced with roots, from the top of which the tree appears to erupt. This mound of roots and mould seems to act as a breathing organ and continuous trampling is now known to have a deleterious effect upon the health of the tree, death being the ultimate result. Kauri produces a gum resin known as copal which is used in paints, varnishes and linoleum. The timber is valued for a variety of purposes.

Below: *Araucaria araucana*
Right: *Agathis australis*

Away across the Pacific in the hills and mountains of Chile and Argentina grows the monkey puzzle or Chile pine (*Araucaria araucana*), surely one of the most improbable of all trees. Straight of bole and having rings of horizontal sturdy branches, arranged with almost mathematical precision, is its basic form. The unique touch is the foliage, which is dark green, tough, leathery and astonishingly long-lived—up to fifteen years—and persists for many years after it ceases to function. These leaves are shield-shaped and spirally arranged just like the scales of an armadillo except that they have a sharp, hard point. Planted in the small gardens of Europe and particularly Britain, as isolated specimens, they look ridiculously out of place. On the rugged volcanic slopes of their Andean homeland they are supremely right, and to wander through a pure forest of them is an experience never to be forgotten.

Having the same branch arrangement, but making a taller more slender tree, is the Norfolk Island pine (*Araucaria heterophylla*, formerly *A. excelsa*). In the wild it is confined to little Norfolk Island which sits well out in the ocean midway between North Island, New Zealand and Brisbane, Australia. Since it was introduced to Europe around 1793, it has been much planted as an ornamental tree, particularly around the Mediterranean. It is also planted in the milder areas of the USA and in Australia and New Zealand. Young plants bear bright green, soft textured, awl-shaped incurved leaves which on young plants create a very decorative plumy effect. For this reason it is much grown in pots for house decoration. Leaves on the adult trees are rather like those of the monkey puzzle in miniature $-\frac{1}{4}$ in long against $1\frac{1}{2}$–2in—and overlap in the same way.

Bunya-bunya is the Australian aboriginal name for *A. bidwillii*, another unique member of this southern hemisphere genus. It grows wild in the Coast District of Queensland, where the aboriginals rely upon it as a food source. They come from miles away each year to gather the nuts and the Australian government has set aside a reserve for this purpose, which comprises a tract of hill country 80 miles long, where tree felling is prohibited. Each tribe has its own trees which are again subdivided among families. The bunya-bunya produces some seeds each year, but only every third year is there a full crop. This is because the huge cones that bear them take three years to ripen. They grow on the uppermost branches and when full sized are larger than a man's head and can weigh 10 lb. The nut-like seeds are pear-shaped, $2-2\frac{1}{2}$ in long by 1 in or more wide. Up to 150 are carried in one cone and represent a valuable source of oil and portein. The tree can reach 150 ft tall and somewhat resembles a monkey puzzle, but the leaves are smaller and narrower and the branchlets more tufted.

Nowadays, the maidenhair tree (*Ginkgo*

biloba) is no longer classified along with the conifers, its ancestry being even more remote. Indeed, direct ancestors were alive before the Jurassic period about 180 million years ago, their fossil remains clearly providing the evidence. The clearest point of difference from the true conifers is the leaf shape, for instead of being narrow or needle-like they are fan-shaped and somewhat resemble the leaflets of the maidenhair fern. Young trees produce a slender spar-like trunk with an irregular collection of short branches, a few of which grow out in an eccentric way to form horizontal 'cross trees'. Eventually more and more of the branches grow out and a heavy head with pendulous tips results. The maidenhair tree stands up well to regular pruning and then forms a bushy but less elegant head much sooner. It is often planted as a street tree in Japan and parts of the USA. The insignificant flowers are borne on separate trees and both sexes are required if the yellowish plum-like fruits are to be seen. When ripe, the fruit falls to the ground and usually ruptures. The flesh is somewhat oily and has an unpleasant rancid odour. Each fruit contains a single stone or seed with a pleasantly edible kernel much appreciated by the Chinese and Japanese, who believe that they suppress the effects of alcohol and aid digestion. No convincingly wild stands of this very ancient tree are known, though there are areas in the Chekiang province of China where many trees

grow spontaneously. This is a tree that relies upon man for survival and most specimens are planted around temples and palaces in China and Japan. Since 1690, when Engelbert Kaempfer first saw it in Japan, and particularly since about 1727 when it was introduced into Europe, it has been spread around the countries of the temperate world where it graces parks and gardens with its attractive foliage, which turns a clear bright yellow in autumn.

Left: *Araucaria excelsa*
Above: Autumn foliage of *Ginkgo biloba*

Maple and Plane

The splendour of autumn across North America, parts of Europe, Asia and particularly Japan, would not be complete without the many kinds of maple (*Acer*). Most of the 200 known species have the characteristic maple leaf typified by Canada's emblem, the sugar maple (*A. saccharum*). This has a leaf basically rounded in outline but cut into three to five, toothed, triangular lobes. Among exceptions to the rule are species with tri-lobed and oval, non-lobed leaves. Most distinctive is that of the box elder or ash-leaved maple (*A. negundo*) which as the latter vernacular name suggests has leaves like that of ash, composed of three to five separate leaflets. A native of North America, where it grows mainly by rivers, streams and lakes, box elder is a small tree, rarely exceeding 30–40 ft. It is much cultivated, especially in Britain.

It is in the autumn, however, that many of the maples come into their own. As the foliage reaches the end of its life, the chlorophyll decomposes and gives way to shades of red, orange and yellow. One of the most spectacular in this respect is the sugar maple (*A. saccharum*). In its native, eastern North America it lights up mile after mile of the woodlands with shades of crimson, orange and gold—a superb sight whether viewed from beneath the tree canopy or hundreds of feet up in an aeroplane. Equally startling is the solid crimson of the red maple (*A. rubrum*), especially those individuals which colour early, while surrounding trees are still green. Also known as the swamp or water maple, owing to its predeliction for wet or moist soils, the red maple is colourful at all times of the year. Early in the year before the leaves expand, the glossy reddish twigs bear fuzzy clusters of small red flowers which, while nothing to see in themselves, bathe the tree in a startling red haze. Later the young leaves appear and with them the fast developing winged seeds (samaras or keys), which also are in shades of red. The leaves gradually turn to bright green, but the seeds stay red until just before they are shed in early summer.

The red and silver maples (*A. saccharinum*) are the only temperate species that flower before the leaves expand and the seeds ripen

in summer. They are borne on the warm summer winds, driven to earth by a sudden thunder shower and quickly germinate, thus gaining a growing season on all the autumn seeding maples. The silver or white maple can reach 60 ft or more in height, but loses nothing in grace. The deeply lobed leaves are jaggedly toothed and borne on long slender stalks which allows them free movement with every breath of wind, revealing the silvery white undersides.

In addition to their attractive foliage, several maples have decorative bark. Most of these are of Asiatic origin, but one North American species stands supreme. This is the moosewood or striped maple (*A. pensylvanicum*), which has smooth, olive green bark, startlingly striated with vein-like, white lines. Although only a small tree, rarely exceeding 25 ft tall, the leaves are large and handsome, bright green with usually only three pointed lobes.

The group of maples with white striped or marbled bark is popularly referred to as the snake barks, owing to the patterned trunks. From Japan comes *A. grosseri* which much resembles moosewood, but with the addition of red and yellow autumn foliage. Neater in habit and smaller in foliage is David's snakebark maple (*A. davidii*) which also colours well in autumn. This is distinctive in having oval, unlobed leaves. A different kind of bark beauty is found in the paperbark maple (*A. griseum*) which has smooth bark that peels away in paper thin strips to reveal a cinnamon surface with a satiny finish. The leaves, which are composed of three oval leaflets, colour well in autumn. Its home is in the mountains of central China.

One of the most popular of all maples in the gardens of the temperate world is surely the Japanese maple (*A. palmatum*). Many forms exist, some of which rarely exceed shrub stature, all colouring magnificently in autumn with leaves of crimson and orange. The wild type comes from China, Korea and Japan where it forms a small, slender twigged tree clad with smooth, five- to seven-lobed, bright green leaves.

A well grown sycamore maple (*A. pseudo-platanus*) can present a magnificent sight with its dense rounded head of dark green foliage, which can top 110 ft or so. The leaves are of typical maple shape, rounded in outline with five to seven lobes bearing small blunt teeth. They are bronze when young and then combine well with the developing pendent clusters of yellow-green flowers. The fruits which follow the flowers have broad wings and are borne far and wide by the autumn gales. Fruits are produced abundantly and the contained seeds germinate readily. Much too readily for the forester who considers this fast growing tree a noxious weed in his plantations. The white to pale yellow wood takes on a satiny finish and is used for furniture, parquet flooring and turnery. It can also be used for making violins.

Left: *Acer saccharum*
Above: *Acer rubrum*
Right: *Acer griseum*

The sycamore is a native of Europe, as is the Norway maple (*A. platanoides*), both having been introduced into North America where they have become locally naturalized. The Norway maple resembles the sugar maple in its leaves, though the large teeth are usually more sharply pointed. A more ready means of differentiating between the two is to snap the leaf stalk of the Norway maple which shows a milky sap. The fruits are a further aid, those of the Norway being larger, the two wings at a 90° angle and the seed end pressed almost flat. It forms a similar tree to the sycamore maple but with a more open and brighter green canopy. In autumn the leaves turn a clear rich yellow and in spring rounded clusters of bright

yellow-green flowers open before the leaves.

Although the various kinds of plane tree have maple-like foliage, they are not in any way botanically related to the true maples. The superficial resemblance is so great however, that it is convenient to deal with them here. Of the ten species of plane tree known, two are outstanding, the oriental plane (*Platanus orientalis*) from south-eastern Europe and the buttonwood or sycamore (*P. occidentalis*) from the central states of the USA. The latter tree has the least maple-like foliage, each massive leaf—up to 9 in across—being roughly pentagonal in outline, pointed at the corners and with wide shallow teeth in between. However, leaves on the same tree can be very variable in both shape and size. Buttonwood is one of the most massive trees in the eastern USA, large specimens attaining 175 ft, with a bole diameter of 12–14 ft. The oriental plane seldom exceeds 100 ft tall and has a rounded head of far flung branches. The leaves are typically maple-like with five prominent lobes. Both trees have an intriguingly crooked branchlet system which identifies them immediately in winter. Both also bear their seeds in hard, ball-shaped clusters, pendulous on wiry stalks and looking like some sort of Christmas decoration as they hang from the bare twigs all winter. In spring each ball breaks up and the seeds, with their tufts of gingery hair are distributed far and wide by the wind. In Europe, particularly in Britain, parts of temperate North and South America, New Zealand and other temperate lands the London plane (*P. x. hispanica* or *P. x. acerifolia*) is often cultivated. It arose as a hybrid between *P. occidentalis* and *P. orientalis* in Europe some time before 1700. It much resembles buttonwood in its tall and stately bearing, but the leaves are very variable and combine characters from both parents. One of the most striking characters is the flaking bark which it gets from the buttonwood parent. As the bark is shed in scale-like patches a mottled pattern of green-white and buff is revealed, which lightens the massive boles in a delightful way.

Top left: Autumn foliage of *Acer palmatum*
Centre left: Autumn foliage of *Acer platanoides*
Bottom left: *Acer pseudoplatanus*
Above: Winter trunk of *Platanus x hispanica*
Right: *Platanus orientalis*

Elm and Lime

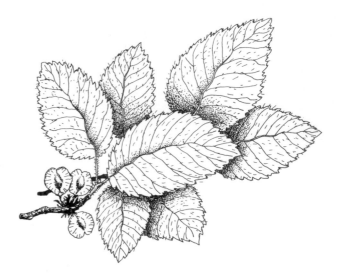

Elms have long held a place of affection in the hearts of British people, particularly those who live in the Midlands and further south where they dominate the landscape. In the USA too, elms are valued and admired, no doubt initially due to the influence of early settlers from southern England. Of the forty-five known species of elm (*Ulmus*), which are scattered across Europe, Asia, Indochina, Mexico and North America, only a handful of species engender this affection. In Britain, *Ulmus procera, glabra, carpinifolia* and hybrids are the main ones, whilst in the USA the American elm (*U. americana*) and the slippery or red elm (*U. rubra*) are the main contenders. When well grown, all are majestic and often lofty trees with rounded heads and grey fissured bark. Their oval, pointed, sharply toothed leaves are characteristically lop-sided, one side being a little longer than the other. All bear tiny petalless flowers with reddish stamens direct from the buds in early spring before the leaves expand. The flowers are followed by oval or rounded fruits which are composed of a central seed and a circular membranous wing which allows distribution by wind. Each seed grows rapidly and the green clusters are often mistaken for young leaves which then mysteriously turn brown and fall just as the true leaves expand. Germination takes place soon after the seeds are shed and the tiny trees may be 18 in tall by the end of the year.

Stateliest of the elms and the one most associated with the English landscape is the aptly named English elm (*Ulmus procera*). Capable of attaining 100 ft or more it characteristically shows a waisted crown, rather like two crowns one above the other. With a more uniformly rounded head is the wych elm (*U. glabra*) having large leaves bearing a striking pattern of deeply embossed parallel veins.

Left: *Ulmus procera*
Right: *Ulmus glabra*

The smooth-leaved elm (*U. carpinifolia*) can usually be identified from a distance, even in winter, by the dense forest of small branchlets that spring straight from the lower trunk, the 'brushwood sheath round the elm tree bole' of Browning. Above this sheath small branches arise and beyond this the rounded to flattish crown of larger branches. Nowhere in the world does it so dominate the landscape as in the Midlands, southern and particularly eastern England. Here it is frequently a hedgerow tree or is the main constituent of copses and woods which scatter the rolling countryside. It is a very variable species and the subject of much taxonomic confusion. The most distinctive variety is *U.c. cornubiensis*, formerly known as *U. stricta* and colloquially as the Cornish elm. It has an erect growth habit and when young to middle-aged is neatly pyramidal. Characteristic of the south-west of England and in the Channel Islands and Brittany, this elm thrives well near the sea and makes an excellent avenue tree. Well grown specimens of the American or white elm (*U. americana*) can attain 125 ft and form wide heads of gracefully spreading branches. A solitary specimen can be a most attractive sight with its canopy of slender-pointed leaves and fissured ash-grey bark. It was formerly common in eastern and central North America, but Dutch elm disease has decimated several of its original sites. All the elms mentioned so far are susceptible to this disease and at the time of writing (1974) fears are great that much of the elm population of southern Britain and parts of Europe will succumb. However, the status of Dutch elm disease ebbs and flows and it is quite possible that this prognostication is unduly pessimistic.

Belonging to the same family as the elms are several species of *Zelkova*, handsome trees with smooth grey bark that later flakes away. *Zelkova serrata* is a native of China, Japan and Korea. It forms a medium-sized tree composed of gracefully wide spreading branches clad with neat oval, slender-pointed leaves. In autumn the foliage takes on bronze and red tints.

From the Caucasus comes *Z. carpinifolia* bearing leaves very like those of hornbeam. In winter the remarkable branch system can be seen and admired to the full. From a short, thick trunk a sheaf of branches arises almost at the same point, some rising vertically others spreading to the side, creating a dense, broadly conical head.

Limes are in no way related to the elms, but they are often planted in our parks and gardens, combine well together and have similar cultural requirements. As a group, the limes (*Tilia*) are typified by pointed, heart-shaped leaves, the rounded lobes at the base often unequally balanced. Several species bear richly fragrant, yellow-green blossoms attached to a leaf-like membranous bract. When the flowers have faded and the small seed capsules are mature the whole cluster and

attached bract fall and are carried by the autumn gales to new sites. The American basswood or linden (*Tilia americana*), also known as the American lime, can reach 130 ft with a trunk diameter of 3 ft or more. It is an imposing tree, the shaft-like stem rising straight up to the round-topped head composed of horizontal branches and weeping branchlets. The smooth red-brown twigs usually zig-zag from bud to bud and the large leaves are very obviously asymmetrical. The light brown wood is straight grained and easily worked, being used for furniture making and turnery. As with all the lime species, the inner bark is very tough and stringy and is still sometimes shredded and used for mat making and cordage. Formerly the bark shreds or bass were much used by nurserymen and gardeners for tying plants but have now been superseded first by raffia and now by plastic tape and string.

From Europe, westwards to the Caucasus, comes the large-leaved lime (*T. platyphyllos*) another fast growing and handsome tree similar to the American lime, but with slender, pointed, dark green leaves that are smooth above and hairy below. The small-leaved lime (*T. cordata*) is even more widely spread in Europe, growing wild as far north as Finland and well into central Russia. It has leaves only half the size of the large-leaved lime, varying from $1\frac{1}{4}-2\frac{1}{2}$ in long, each one being dark shining green above and pale green beneath, bearing a blue-white patina. Reaching 75 ft or more in height, it has a somewhat less spreading habit than the foregoing species and makes a good avenue tree. Green tinted, ivory flowers appear in late July and are eagerly sought after by honey bees.

Known variously as the common lime, linden or lind, *Tilia x europaea* is a hybrid between the large- and small-leaved limes and blends the characters of both. In Europe it is the most commonly planted lime tree particularly in parks and as avenues. It has a more tapered head of branches than its parents but this touch of elegance is often spoilt by dense, brushy suckers from the lower trunk. A fragrant tea can be brewed from the dried blossoms, and the fresh flowers —via the honey-bee—yield a delicious, delicately flavoured honey.

Top left: *Ulmus americana*
Bottom left: *Zelkova carpinifolia*
Top right: Foliage and fruits of *Tilia cordata*
Bottom right: *Zelkova serrata*
Overleaf: *Tilia x europaea*

Ash, Beech, Oak

In both Europe and North America, and indeed in much of temperate Asia as well, the various species of ash, beech and oak are among the most popular and useful of all the hardwood trees. Beech and oak are botanically closely related, being members of the same family. Ash, on the other hand, belongs to the olive family and is thus related to such popular shrubs as lilac, forsythia and jasmine. Apart from a few unusual forms and varieties, all the seventy known species of ash have compound leaves composed of several distinct, oval, pointed leaflets arranged in opposite pairs. Most species bear insignificant, fuzzy clusters of greenish or yellowish flowers on the bare stems in spring. There are also a few species

which bear large heads of white or cream flowers with the bright green young leaves. These are known as flowering ashes, the best being the manna ash (*Fraxinus ornus*), a round headed tree barely exceeding 60 ft and often much less. It is widespread in parts of southern Europe and adjacent western Asia, often growing on the rocky hillsides overlooking the sea, where it lends character and beauty to the spring-time scene. Much rarer in the wilds of southern Europe eastwards to Iran and Turkestan is the small and graceful *F. oxycarpa* with neat small leafage which takes on pleasing shades of purple.

The commonest and best known and loved of the European ashes is the aptly named

common ash (*F. excelsior*). Growing in the open it forms a massive round-headed tree, but among other trees it can soar up to 150 ft with a straight, little branched, grey barked bole. It is one of the latest trees to leaf in the spring, usually May having all but passed before there is a good head of foliage. The leaves, which are composed of nine to fifteen leaflets, also fall earlier than most other trees. Sometimes the tree is bare again only five months after the leaves have expanded. But whether clothed in its light canopy of leaves or showing its distinctive tracery of sturdy, black-budded twigs in winter, this is an appealing tree and most handsome when well grown. Long before the leaves appear, the twigs of mature trees are garlanded with fluffy clusters of tiny flowers with reddish stamens. Later the characteristic winged fruits appear, slender and twisted just like half of an aeroplane propeller. Like the fruits of the sycamore maple, they are also known as keys or samaras.

Crossing the Atlantic we come upon a very similar tree, the white ash (*F. americana*). It can be easily distinguished from the common ash by its leaves, which have only five to nine leaflets, and winter twigs with brown buds. Like the common ash it is fast growing and has strong resilient wood, much favoured for making the handles of tools and particularly horticultural and agricultural implements. It is also used to make oars and for the interior finish of houses.

Known alternatively as brown or river ash, the red ash (*F. pensylvanica*) is a closely related tree widely distributed in the eastern part of North America, where it tends to inhabit river banks, the margins of ponds and swamps and other areas of rich, moist soil. Its vernacular name is derived from the terra-cotta colouring of the under surfaces of the bark on the branches. An attractive ash from the western side of the USA is *F. latifolia* (*F. oregona*), locally known as the Oregon ash. A robust, stout twigged species with large hairy leaves, it can attain 75 ft and forms a prominent feature of its canyon homeland in the Sierra Nevada and coast ranges of California.

There are no less than 450 different kinds of oak ranging in size from low scrub a foot or so tall to trees of 160 ft or more; some are evergreen, the rest deciduous. Among this assemblage there are some of the most valuable, broadleaved timber trees of the temperate world. Several also are of noble appearance or take on bright tints in autumn.

Left: *Fraxinus ornus*
Below: *Fraxinus excelsior*

Having close historical associations, the common or English oak (*Quercus robur*) is widespread in Europe extending southwards to North Africa and eastwards to the Caucasus. It is a sturdy tree with a wide spreading, rounded crown of crooked branches that create a fascinating winter silhouette. The oval leaves, rather broader at the tip, are cut into irregular rounded lobes. They seem to provide a basic pattern for many oak species or at least a theme upon which there are endless variations. Although such a familiar sight and seldom looked upon as anything out of the ordinary, the fruit of the oak, known as an acorn in English speaking countries, is a unique object; an egg-shaped, nut-like seed,

sitting naked in a neat, little scaly bowl like an egg in an egg cup. They appear to be unpromising units of propagation, lacking wings, tufts of hair or hooks to aid distribution. Birds and such animals as squirrels help to move them away from the parent tree, and gale tossed branches can catapult them a surprising distance. Even so it is astonishing how widespread the oaks are.

The common oak and its close ally, the sessile oak (*Q. petraea*) have a fine grained, strong, hard, heart wood that has been much in demand since earliest times for boat building, high quality furniture, parquet flooring and barrel-making to mention but a few of its uses. Its bark is rich in tannin and

was formerly much used in tanneries. Several interesting forms have arisen by mutation and are grown in parks and gardens. The fern-leaved oak has the leaves divided into slender segments; the cypress oak grows in a narrow column; and the weeping oak has pendulous branches. There is also one with purple leaves.

Taller and rather more graceful, but in a very masculine way, is the Turkey oak (*Q. cerris*), which inhabits southern Europe and western Turkey. Its leaves are longer than the common oak and rather more jaggedly lobed. Most distinctive is the acorn cup which is loosely covered with small cylindrical scales like coarse moss.

The holm or evergreen oak (*Q. ilex*) is a characteristic tree of the Mediterranean area and south-western Europe, where it is an important shade and timber tree. Its richly green glossy leaves are variable in shape. On young trees and saplings they often resemble holly (*Ilex aquifolium*), but on mature specimens they are unlobed and almost elliptic.

Still of great economic importance in Spain and Portugal, despite the advent of plastics, is the cork oak (*Q. suber*). Rather similar to the holm oak and also evergreen this tree is clearly distinguished by its thick and firmly, spongy, deeply fissured and convoluted bark. This is stripped off when it reaches a usable thickness and is the raw material for all the objects made of cork. Across the ocean in the south-eastern USA is another evergreen species of similar appearance to the holm oak, known as the live oak (*Q. virginiana*). Its small, elliptic to oblong, leathery leaves are toothless and provide welcome shade during the long hot summers of that region. It is often festooned in a most picturesque way with the grey beards of Spanish moss.

In favourable situations, the white oak (*Q. alba*) can attain 150 ft tall and a bole diameter of 3 ft. This massively handsome species is so named because of its whitish bark and grey twigs. It is of great economic value in its native, eastern North American homeland, the wood having the same uses as the common

Above left: *Quercus robur*
Above right: Foliage and fruit of *Quercus cerris*
Above centre: *Quercus ilex*
Below right: *Quercus suber* (with its trunk stripped of cork)

oak. Much planted for the cardinal red of its dying leaves, the scarlet oak (*Q. coccinea*) also comes from the eastern parts of North America. It belongs to that group of oaks with large, narrow lobes to the leaves, usually bearing bristle points. Only a little less decorative is the red oak (*Q. rubra*) with larger leaves that turn maroon-red in autumn. It can be a massive tree attaining, under ideal conditions, 140 ft, with a bole diameter of 6 ft.

Similar, but usually much smaller and neatly pyramidal when young, is the pin or swamp oak (*Q. palustris*) with deeply lobed leaves that also turn a good red in autumn. It has an almost globular acorn which looks faintly ridiculous sitting in the shallowest of saucer-like cups. Much in contrast is the acorn of the chestnut or rock oak (*Q. prinus*) whose glossy, chestnut-red, torpedo shape is nearly half enclosed in a deep, nobbly, scaled cup. This fine oak comes from the dry hillsides and rocky woods in North America, north to Lake Erie and west to Kentucky. It is further distinguished by very large and shallowly lobed leaves up to 7 in long.

Up in the Sierra Nevada of California grows the California black oak (*Q. kelloggii*) often in company with the incense cedar and other conifers, its glossy, deeply lobed leaves making a striking contrast of form and even more so with the black tracery of its winter twigs.

To wander in a forest of well grown, common beech trees (*Fagus sylvatica*), either in winter or summer is a most satisfying experience. In winter the smooth grey trunks rise up to an elegant tracery of slender zig-zag twigs spiked with slim, pointed buds. In summer, the same column-like boles soar into a canopy of rich green foliage, which effectively keeps out the heat of the hottest summer day. Many people have likened a beech forest to an open-air cathedral and there is no doubt that the air of quiet serenity on a calm summer's day can have a most soothing effect on the mind. In open parkland, the common beech assumes more massive proportions, the broad rounded head of branches supported by a low and heavily branched trunk. The branchlets bear rows of twigs on either side, forming frond-like sprays of great charm, particularly in spring, when the somewhat glossy, bright, luminous green, oval leaves unfold.

Above left: *Quercus palustris*
Below left: *Quercus kelloggii*
Right: *Fagus sylvatica*

Later in the year these leaves mature to a rich full green. Tiny pompon-like flower clusters of greenish flowers appear with the young leaves, the males dangling on long, slender stalks, the females on shorter, sturdier ones. In autumn, the latter appear as hard, woody cups with four, tightly closed, petal-like segments, which protect the sharply triangular nutlets. These are much sought after by squirrels and other small rodents when the cups are opened by the drying, early autumn winds. Also known as mast, the nutlets are pleasantly edible and nutritious and yield a good quality oil. Good mast years are of irregular occurrence and seem to rely upon warm summer weather the previous year which ripens the stems and initiates flower buds. It is well worthwhile sowing a few nutlets in autumn to observe the curious un-beech-like seedlings that emerge the following spring. These have two, fleshy, seed leaves which are broadly fan-shaped and faintly grooved and crimped. From between them in due course a pair of recognizable beech leaves develop. The common beech is native to Europe, ranging from Britain and northern Spain eastwards to the Black Sea. It is one of the few broadleaved, temperate trees to form pure forests. Owing to its majestic appearance it has been much planted in parks and large gardens.

There are several decorative, cultivated sorts notably the copper, red and purple-leaved ones, grouped under the subspecies *F. s. purpurea*. Like the original species, these variants turn a splendid copper gold as the leaves die in autumn. The strong, heavy, attractively mottled wood has many uses, including butter casks, furniture and articles of kitchen and table use. The American beech (*F. grandifolia*) is a rather similar tree, but easily distinguished by its toothed leaves, which are slender, pointed and much longer—up to 5 in as against the $3\frac{1}{2}$ in maximum of the common beech. It is a native of the richer, moister, upland soils in the eastern USA and adjacent Canada, where it can produce massive specimens more than 100 ft in height.

In autumn it is particularly effective as the leaves gradually turn to pale gold and then to pale buff. Quite often the leaves remain on the tree well into the winter, brightening the gloom of grey cold days.

At one time included in the same genus as beech are a group of trees from the southern hemisphere, now commonly known as southern beeches (*Nothofagus*—from the Greek 'nothos', meaning false). Some thirty-five species are known, mainly from the mountains of temperate South America and Australasia where they sometimes form vast pure forests. One of the most spectacular in this respect is *N. solandri*, in its native New Zealand known as black beech. In the Southern Alps, as one journeys over Arthur's Pass for example, the steep mountain slopes are covered, mile after mile, with the deep glossy green of countless millions of small gnarled trees. Up near the limit of tree growth they are little more than wind blown shrubs, but in more sheltered lowland habitats specimens of 80 ft can occasionally be found.

The black beech is one of the evergreen members of its genus and bears tiny box-like leaves rarely more than $\frac{1}{2}$ in long. In the form *N. s. cliffortioides* (mountain beech) they may be even smaller and are curiously folded and twisted. The silver beech (*N. menziesii*) has rounded, prettily notched and glossy, ever-green leaves that seldom exceed $\frac{1}{3}$ in long. It is also a New Zealander and can be found in

lowland and mountain woods but usually mixed with other tree species. In sheltered spots it can reach 90 ft or more with a hand-some grey-white to silvery bole.

Even taller is the red beech (*N. fusca*) with oval, prominently toothed, 1 in long leaves that rather resemble those of a small elm or hornbeam. A shapely specimen standing in a woodland clearing can be a splendid sight, the lofty head supported on a dark, often buttressed, trunk, bearing thick, furrowed bark. The common name is gained from the wood which is dark red when freshly sawn.

Across the Pacific from New Zealand grows the roble beech (*N. obliqua*), a deciduous

species growing up to 100 ft, which inhabits mountains in Chile. It is a fast growing tree and has been tried out for forestry purposes in other parts of the temperate world, notably in Britain. The oval leaves are neatly and shallowly lobed, each lobe bearing three small teeth. Like most of the other southern beeches the triangular woody fruits contain three nutlets, two triangular and one flattened ovoid between them.

Left: *Fagus grandifolia*
Above: *Nothofagus solandri*
Below: Foliage and fruits of *Nothofagus menziesii*

Birch, Alder, Hornbeam

Next to the oak and beech, the birch is probably the most easily recognized of trees. No less than sixty species of birch are known, all from northern temperate regions, where they often inhabit heathland, moorland or mountain slopes. In Europe, the most characteristic one is the common or silver birch (*Betula pendula*), which has a silvery white trunk and slender, wiry branchlets, which on mature specimens hang gracefully down. Elegance is the hallmark of this tree and it well merits the alternative vernacular in Britain of 'Lady of the Woods'. In winter, the dangling clusters of small branchlets and twigs resemble tresses of hair as they swing to and fro in the wind. The almost triangular leaves, sharply toothed and slender pointed, also tend to hang down and create a light canopy which allows plenty of dappled light to come through. In spring as the leaves unfold, yellow male and tiny green female catkins appear. Wind carries the dust-like pollen to the female flowers which then slowly transform into small, sausage-shaped 'cones'. Later, these dry up and fall apart, releasing many, tiny, winged nutlets or seeds. The seed crop from an average sized tree is prodigious and one lone specimen at the edge of a woodland glade or moorland tract can soon give rise to a forest of seedlings. The silver birch is much planted for ornamental purposes and the tough wood has been used for furniture, veneers and skis, the twigs for broom making and the bark for tanning leather.

From China comes the beautiful *B. albo-sinensis* which has pink and red bark overlaid with a waxy blue-white patina. It has an equally fetching variety, *B. albo-sinensis septentrionalis* which has bright orange-brown bark overlaid with pinkish grey.

Right: *Betula pendula*
Above right: *Betula ermanii*
Above far right: *Betula albo-sinensis*
Below far right: *Betula papyrifera*

From the mountains of Japan and the adjacent mainland of Asia originates Erman's birch (*B. ermanii*). in its best forms it can rival *B. albo-sinensis*, having a pinkish-white trunk and orange-brown branches, set off by glossy rich green foliage.

The most common and beautiful birch of the northern USA and most of Canada is the paper or canoe birch (*B. papyrifera*). Combining elegance with height—it can reach 100 ft—this tree has a startling, chalky white trunk, which separates into aromatic papery layers. The large oval leaves are often somewhat heart-shaped at the base and turn clear yellow in autumn. In late winter, a cut branch will yield abundant sweetish sap which can be made into a beer or wine. Pale brown, hard and close grained, the wood is used for turnery and wood pulp. The durable waterproof bark was once extensively used by the Indians to make canoes.

Allied to the birches are the various species of alder (*Alnus*), several of which are characteristic of river or lake sides or swampy ground. The grey, hoary or speckled alder (*A. incana*) has a very wide natural range, occurring in Europe, Asia and North America. Generally a smallish tree of about 30 ft, though rarely almost twice this, the grey alder frequently grows as a cluster of small erect trunks bearing many, small, spreading branches. The hairy twigs bear broadly oval leaves that are greyish on the under surface and a rich matt green above. The purple and yellow, male catkins are very conspicuous, borne as they are on naked twigs in late winter. Smaller, ovoid, female catkins turn into woody cones, which strongly resemble those of coniferous trees. When they ripen, tiny winged nutlets fall and are carried far and wide on strong winds. The grey alder is tolerant of a wide variety of soil conditions, but thrives best in moist but not waterlogged conditions.

The common alder (*A. glutinosa*) on the other hand is seen at its best by rivers and lakes. It is widespread in Europe and extends eastwards to the Caucasus and Siberia. It is usually taller than *A. incana* and can attain up to 70 ft. Until old it has a central trunk rather like that of many conifers, with small horizontally borne branches. The reddish catkins expand in spring before the leaves. When freshly cut the timber is yellow-white but soon turns brick red. It is used for turnery, clogs, window frames and pencils, and takes paint and varnish well.

The hornbeams (*Carpinus*) are sometimes confused with the beeches, but their leaves are narrower and more prominently veined. Most distinctive of all are the small, nut-like fruits which are attached to leafy, three-lobed wings. The American hornbeam (*C. carolinianus*) is also known in its nativeland as the blue or water beech, names that reflect its slate-grey trunk and predilection for wet areas. Usually a small tree under 30 ft the blue beech has oval, toothed and pointed leaves

often somewhat asymmetrical at the base.

Much more majestic in every way is the common hornbeam of Europe and the Caucasus (*C. betulus*). In an open site it forms a round-headed tree composed of a flattened branchlet system similar to the beech. The smooth bark is fawn and grey and a cross-section of the trunk reveals an oval or irregular outline. In spring the yellowish, male catkins appear with the young leaves. Wind-blown pollen finds its way to the tiny, green female catkins which later become 'leafy' and rather like elongated hops. When ripe, each small, ribbed nut and its attached wing separate and can be carried great distances on the autumn gales. Beam is derived from the German 'Baum' which means tree, thus hornbeam describes a tree like horn or with horny wood. The name is apt, for the timber is tough, hard and heavy. It was formerly used for making the cogwheels in mills and is still used for tool handles, wooden screws and rollers.

Closely allied are the hop hornbeams (*Ostrya*), the best known being the American hop horn-beam (*O. caroliniana*), also known as ironwood and leverwood in its native eastern USA and adjacent Canada. As the common name suggests, the fruiting clusters are just like those of the hop, being composed of oval, inflated bracts, each one containing a small nut. Like that of hornbeam, the wood is very hard and strong and is used for the same purposes. The common hop hornbeam (*O. carpinifolia*) like the common hornbeam is a finer tree than its American counterpart, making a handsome, round-headed tree up to 60 ft or more. It is a native of southern Europe and Asia Minor, where it inhabits mountain ranges or the higher hills, sometimes, as around Lake Como, forming woods of considerable extent.

Left: Catkins and last year's fruits of *Alnus glutinosa*
Above right: *Carpinus betulus*
Below right: Male and female catkins of *Carpinus betulus*

Poplar and Willow

Variously known as poplars, cottonwoods and aspens, most of the species in the genus *Populus* are fast growing trees which thrive best in moist soil. In the wild they are often found by streams and lakes or grow on mountain slopes which enjoy a fairly high rainfall. Poplar wood is rather woolly in texture and light in weight. It has no odour and so is in demand for food containers and is used extensively for making chip baskets for packing fruit and other eatables. The main demand however for the wood is for the making of matches and match boxes. Much of the poplar wood used comes from planted trees of hybrid origin. These are very fast growing and can yield logs of 60–70 ft after only twenty years of growth. Poplars fall roughly into two groups, the true poplars and cottonwoods with triangular or heart-shaped leaves and the aspens and white poplars with oval or rounded ones, usually variously toothed or lobed.

The common aspen (*P. tremula*) has a wide distribution in Europe, north to Iceland, and across Asia as far as Japan. It even crosses the Mediterranean into Algeria. The pale green leaves have neatly scalloped margins and endlessly flutter on slender, ribbon-flat stalks. In early spring, before the leaves expand, thick furry catkins unfurl looking just like caterpillars. In autumn the leaves often turn a clear yellow. This is a suckering tree rarely exceeding 60 ft, and more often forming thickets of half this height.

Its North American cousin (*P. tremuloides*) is a similar but more attractive tree with smaller marginal crenellations to the leaves and a smooth trunk, which can vary from chalk-white to yellow-green. In autumn the leaves change to a bright clear yellow and are a real feature of the dry slopes and mountains it inhabits. It ranges south to the mountains of Mexico and north to Alaska where it is

Left: *Populus tremuloides*
Centre: *Populus alba*
Right: *Populus fremontii*

sometimes also called the popple. The wood is sometimes used for the interior finish of houses, and extensively for wood pulp. The large-toothed or big-tooth aspen (*P. grandidentata*) is also North American, but largely restricted to the north-eastern states and adjacent Canada. It has handsome leaves up to 5 in long, margined with large, lobe-like teeth. It has been tried as an ornamental in several European countries, but for some unknown reason it rarely thrives for long.

The abele, white or silver poplar (*P. alba*) is a native of Europe and Asia and is commonly planted in America. Its lobed, often almost maple-like leaves are densely white felted beneath and present a striking appearance when endlessly turned to and fro by the summer breezes. All the poplars bear their tiny seeds in scraps of floss-like down, hence the American name cottonwood. This name is however usually applied to various species of the true poplars, foremost among them being the common cottonwood (*P. deltoides*) also known as the Carolina poplar and necklace poplar. The latter vernacular name refers to the necklace-like, fruiting catkins with their small bead-shaped capsules just before they burst to release the cottony seeds. In North America it is widespread in the states east of the Rocky Mountains, south to Florida and north to Quebec, where it inhabits river valleys, stream banks and other moist spots. The Fremont cottonwood (*P. fremontii*) is akin to the Carolina poplar but with a picturesquely leaning trunk and thick, wide, spreading branches bearing slightly smaller, more rounded leaves, But probably the most strikingly handsome of all the poplars is the Chinese, *P. lasiocarpa*, introduced to cultivation in the West as recently as 1904. It forms a round-headed specimen tree, which can reach 60 ft in height but is usually less, clad with massive, red stalked leaves, which may easily be 1 ft long.

Several of the true poplars are permeated with a fragrant oily resin and are known as balsam poplars, the fragrance being like that given off by the balsam fir (*Abies balsamea*). This balsam scent is particularly strong in spring when the fresh, green, young leaves are expanding and can be detected downwind, several hundred yards away. The main balsam poplar, sometimes known also by its Indian name of 'tacamahac', (*P. balsamea*) grows from Newfoundland west to the Hudson Bay and Alaska, south to the Black Hills and northern New England. It can make a finely proportioned tree up to 90 ft, having glistening, tan-brown shoots and lustrous, green leaves that are silvery beneath.

The related, black cottonwood (*P. trichocarpa*) is similar and almost equally fragrant of balsam. It is often cultivated in European gardens, particularly in Britain, but is rather prone to a canker disease of the trunk and branches. It is native to the western seaboard states of North America and Canada.

The leaves of this handsome poplar vary with the altitude at which it grows. When at its altitudinal limit of about 9,000 ft, the leaves become lance-shaped and little more than $\frac{3}{4}$ in wide.

There are no less than 500 species in the willow genus (*Salix*) but comparatively few are large trees. It is in fact a very varied group containing tiny, prostrate, alpine shrublets, medium to large shrubs and trees up to 80 ft tall. The most eye-catching member of this latter group is the white willow (*Salix alba*). In Europe and particularly Britain it is a characteristic tree of river and canal banks, often in its mop-headed, pollarded form, having had the branches removed to promote the growth of pliable young stems for making baskets and hurdles. When allowed to grow naturally it forms a tree with ascending branches which lights up the landscape as the summer breezes ruffle the slender, silvery-white-backed leaves. The cricket bat willow (*S. alba coerulea*) arose as a mutant of the white willow in Britain. It has a somewhat more elegant, pyramidal growth habit and the leaves have a silver-blue cast. The wood is considered the best for making cricket bats and the tree is much cultivated for this purpose.

The crack willow (*S. fragilis*) grows in similar moist places but has a broader, more spreading crown and mid-green leaves. The vernacular name refers to the extremely brittle nature of the twig bases which readily snap when only gently pulled back. The Pekin willow (*S. matsudana*) is a native of northern China, Manchuria and Korea and forms a pleasing tree of pyramidal habit with bright green, narrow leaves. In gardens it is often represented by its mutant form 'Tortuosa' which has the twigs and branchlets curled and twisted in the most peculiar way. This is seen at its best in winter, when the patterned tracery of twigs seen against a blue sky takes on a certain bizarre beauty. In gardens the most familiar kinds of willow are those with a weeping form. The common weeping willow is usually called *S. babylonica*, but it is often confused with *S. x. chrysocoma*, a hybrid between *S. babylonica* and *S. alba*. Both have broad, dome-shaped heads of widely spreading branches which bear vertically hanging branchlets and twigs. True *S. babylonica* has brown twigs and the hybrid has yellow ones. Despite the name, *S. babylonica* comes from China. It was very early on introduced into western Asia, eastern Europe and then western Europe and later to the Americas. The bark of many willow species yields salicylic acid which has similar properties to quinine and is the active pain-killing principal in aspirin.

Left: *Populus trichocarpa*
Top right: Pollarded *Salix fragilis*
Bottom right: *Salix x chrysocoma*

Eucalyptus

Outside the tropics, the various kinds of *Eucalyptus* are the quickest growing and among the tallest of the broadleaved trees. Most of the 500 species are native to Australia where they are found in a wide range of habitats from sea-level to mountain slopes. A curious characteristic shared by many species is the extremely different types of foliage as they grow from seed to maturity. In the most extreme examples the leaves of the juvenile phase are wider than long and spread sideways to link up with its fellow on the other side of the twig. The result appears as a single, circular leaf, pierced by the twig. Young, wand-like shoots are fascinating and highly decorative, threaded, as they appear to be,

with blue-green disk leaves. This juvenile phase can be maintained by constantly cutting the young shoots which creates bushes rather than trees. The cut stems are much in demand by florists, particularly in Britain and parts of the USA.

Known in its native Australia as mountain ash, *Eucalyptus regnans* holds the record as the world's tallest broadleaved tree. It has a fairly limited distribution in Victoria and Tasmania, where it inhabits mountain slopes and valleys which experience cool to mild summers and wet, cold winters. The great columnar trunks of mountain ash are remarkably smooth and white or pale grey in hue. To wander in a forest of these giants set off among elegant tree

ferns is a memorable sight. The timber has a straight grain and is hard and durable, thus making it one of Australia's most valuable timber trees.

Left: *Eucalyptus niphophila*
Right: *Eucalyptus pauciflora*

Owing to the resin which eucalypts produce, many species have vernacular names which include the word gum. Snow gum (*E. niphophila*) is one of these. It is also a mountain tree, inhabiting the snow line altitudes in Victoria and New South Wales. At the limit of tree vegetation this gum takes on a curiously attractive and contorted form, the smooth barked branches writhing in all directions. As the bark peels, splashes of brown, old-gold and sienna show up in a startling way, particularly when contrasted against the blue-white snow.

The white sally (*E. pauciflora*) is a related species with a wider distribution which includes Tasmania. It is a mountain species but never gets as high as the snow gum. It can, under ideal conditions develop into a quite large, spreading tree with glossy, dark red to orange-yellow twigs.

The best known gum tree is *E. globulus*, the Tasmanian blue gum, which has been planted throughout the milder parts of the temperate world. Extremely fast growing—6 ft in a year is not unusual—it soon makes a large tree of handsome appearance with white twigs and dark, glossy green leaves like curved knife blades. The juvenile phase is particularly attractive, the oval, pointed, stem-clasping leaves being a bright blue-green. Seedling plants are often used to combine with brightly coloured annual flowers in the bedding schemes so popular in public parks. The petal-less flowers are composed of a powder-puff-like head of deep stamens. They are attractive creations and it is not surprising that they were chosen as Tasmania's national flower. It is also an important timber tree in that island, growing in wet hill country, usually on the richer soils. Well grown specimens can attain more than 200 ft with a straight columnar trunk bearing a shredding bark patched blue-grey or grey.

Left: *Eucalyptus globulus*
Right: *Eucalyptus camaldulensis*

In Australia itself, the best known and most widespread eucalyptus is the river red gum (*E. camaldulensis*). It is a tree of variable appearance, but in its most typical form is large and gnarled, somewhat like a common oak. It grows in all the states of Australia (except Tasmania) where it is a characteristic tree of dry, open country following water courses (often dry) and the banks of rivers and streams. It so often features in the work of artists and photographers that it has almost become the tree symbol of the Australian landscape.

The ghost gum (*E. papuana*) is widely distributed in northern Australia. It also grows near Port Moresby in Papua, hence its specific botanic name. Well grown specimens have a straight, glossy white trunk and a spreading head of willow-like leaves supported on equally white branches. It often springs out of flat or rolling red rock or soil country and contrasts in a striking and beautiful way. For this reason it has appealed to the landscape painter and in particular has achieved immortality in the brush strokes of aboriginal artists. Most of the eucalypts have white or cream flowers which are not particularly showy unless very profusely borne.

One very noteworthy exception is the red flowering gum (*E. ficifolia*) which is much planted in the warmer parts of the temperate zone as an ornamental. It forms a fairly small, round-headed tree, clad with lance-shaped, leathery textured leaves, which at flowering time become overwhelmed by multitudes of frothy red blossoms. The wild trees bear vermilion flowers, but it has been hybridized with the related marri (*E. calophylla*) to give rise to a wide range of shades from pink to red. Red flowering gum is a rare tree in the wild, being restricted to a few localities in Western Australia.

Below: Flowers of *Eucalyptus ficifolia*
Right: *Eucalyptus papuana*

Chestnut, Walnut, Wingnut

There is much justification for considering the horse chestnut (*Aesculus hippocastanum*) the most majestic and eye-catching of all the hardy forest trees, not withstanding the claims of the tree-sized magnolias. Sturdy of bole and with numerous ascending limbs that can top 100 ft, it forms a high domed crown often with the outermost, lower branchlets pendulous. Throughout the winter, the large glistening ovoid buds are clearly visible and frequently cut for ornamentation as 'sticky buds'. During mild days in March they expand rapidly and during April the felted young leaves emerge and hang down like folded hands. Soon the leaves open out to disclose five to seven leaflets, radiating from the leaf stalk like the

fingers of a hand. In May conical clusters of white flowers expand, standing erect from the the twig tips like fat candles. Flowering is usually profuse and a large tree in full bloom is a sight to behold. Were it a rare tree, surely there would be pilgrimages to see them at blossom time. Individual flowers have an almost orchid-like quality when viewed close to. The petals are crimped, waved and overlap from a short tube. Each bears a lemon-yellow blotch which, as it ages, and as if by some alchemy, gradually turns red. Later, the familiar, spiky, ball-shaped fruits develop, eventually splitting open to disclose the nuts or conkers, grained and polished like the finest mahogany. The horse chestnut is a native to

Albania and Greece but has been extensively planted as an ornamental tree in our parks and gardens.

In the USA there are several species of *Aesculus*, known colloquially as buckeyes. The most decorative of these is the red buckeye (*A. pavia*), a small neat tree which bears rich crimson blossoms followed by smooth fruits. Crossed with the horse chestnut it has given rise to the familiar red horse chestnut of our gardens (*A. x. carnea*), a round-headed tree with profuse pink blossoms in the same style.

Against the lofty peaks of the Himalayas grows the tallest of the genus *Aesculus*, the Indian horse chestnut (*A. indica*). Abundant in the forests on the slopes of the Himalayas

from Nepal to the Indus river this fine tree can attain 150 ft and more with a bole girth of enormous size—40 ft being recorded. It rather resembles a taller, more oval-headed horse chestnut and bears longer, but looser clusters of flowers, the lower two petals of which flush pink. Its particular value as a garden ornament is a later flowering period, from early June to late July, and which follows on from the common horse chestnut.

In no way related, but bearing burr-like fruits and polished nuts, are the true or sweet chestnuts (*Castanea*). Unlike the horse chestnut, the sweet kinds are highly edible and much sought after by man and many animals. The common sweet chestnut (*C. sativa*) is a native of southern Europe eastwards to the Casucasus and has been much planted elsewhere. It is reputed to have been planted in Britain by the Romans and is now partially naturalized in a few places. The large leaves are oval, boldly toothed and veined and form a rich green mantle to a long-headed tree, capable of reaching over 100 ft. Mature specimens have a thick brown bark with very regular, deep, parallel fissures that often curve round the trunk as though some giant hands had given it a half twist. Yellowish-white, bottle-brush-like catkins appear in July to be followed by very spiny, ball-shaped fruits in autumn. Sweet chestnut wood is hard and very durable outside and is much used for fencing. American chestnut (*C. dentata*) is a similar tree but with somewhat narrower leaves and nuts, which are considered to be of a superior flavour. It was once a common tree in its eastern American homeland but has suffered a fungal disease of such severity that few good specimens now remain. Epidemic diseases are rare among trees, but unfortunately this one of chestnuts and the current one of elms are attacking popular and picturesque groups important to their particular landscapes.

Left: Foliage of *Aesculus hippocastanum*
Above right: *Aesculus x carnea*
Right: Catkins and young foliage of *Juglans regia*

Along with almonds and Brazil nuts, walnuts are among the most popular in temperate countries, especially at Christmas time. Such are their popularity that several improved forms have been selected and are grown on an orchard scale in parts of the USA and southern Europe. The common walnut (*Juglans regia*) is the species grown for nuts. It is also a source of valuable timber used for high class furniture and wooden tableware. It is also much used for veneer work to cover the cheaper woods, having a fine polished and attractively grained surface. The walnut is also a very handsome tree, especially when grown as a park specimen with plenty of room to expand. It then forms a wide and ascending crown up to 100 ft supported by a sturdy bole, which is silvery grey in young trees, darker and fissured when older. The large leaves—up to 10 in long—are composed of several smooth, thick textured, oblong to oval leaflets borne on robust twigs. Tiny male flowers are crowded into pendulous greenish catkins. Female flowers have neither petals nor sepals and look like tiny gooseberries with a pair of large, purple, feathery stigmas at the top. These soon grow into large, green, plum-like fruits which, when ripe, split irregularly to disclose the familiar corrugated, pale brown shelled nut.

An equally handsome tree is the black walnut, which can attain, when favourably situated, 150 ft and a bole girth of up to 20 ft.

Its homeland is the richer, moister soils of the eastern USA and adjacent Canada, where it is also a valuable timber tree. In the past it has been much exploited by lumbermen and large specimens are difficult to find. In some areas it was virtually exterminated by felling and, though regeneration has taken place, 80 years are required before the trees are large enough for good timber.

A long-headed tree, the black walnut (*J. nigra*) is easily distinguished from the common sort by its longer leaves composed of eleven to seventeen, narrow, pointed leaflets. The nut is richly flavoured, but the rough, ridged shell is so thick and stone-like that the kernel is almost impossible to extract. Less decorative as a tree is the butternut or white walnut (*J. cinerea*). A broad, spreading tree, occasionally up to 90 ft, it lacks symmetry, with rough, craggy limbs and rather sparse foliage. Nevertheless, a solitary specimen standing at the edge of a wood or corner of a pasture can be a striking and imposing sight in its rough-hewn way. The leaves are composed of seven to seventeen leaflets, usually eleven, each one broadly lance-shaped and slender pointed. Like the black walnut it is a native of the eastern USA but extending only as far south as Georgia and Alabama. When ripe, the ovoid nuts are sweet and edible, but very oily and not much eaten except by small boys. Formerly they were an item of diet of the native Indians.

Closely related to the walnuts are the various kinds of hickory and pecan, also natives of North America. Best known of all is the pecan (*Carya illinoensis*) famed for its oval, lustrous tan brown, thin shelled nuts with crisp, sweet, delicately flavoured kernels. The walnut-like leaves are composed of nine to fifteen asymmetrical, narrowly ovate, finely toothed leaflets, which turn yellow in autumn. The pecan is a tall slender tree, commonly 70–80 ft tall and rarely twice this, which occurs frequently on the moister soils in the mid-eastern states. It is also much cultivated for the nuts and several selected sorts are grown in eastern and western America.

Shagbark hickory is the unprepossessing name applied to *Carya ovata*, probably the most beautiful member of its genus. A large tree with wide spreading boughs, it can attain up to 90 ft, though is usually a little less, with leaves made up of five to seven large leaflets. The vernacular name refers to the shaggy trunk which appears to be roughly thatched with strips of shredded bark. In autumn, the leaves turn a clear, bright yellow which takes on a luminous quality in the evening light. Shagbark produces the commonest hickory nut of the market, a thin-shelled, buff-white, flattened nut with a sweet kernel.

We need to journey to the Black Sea coast and adjacent areas, including the Caucasus, to see the Caucasian wingnut (*Pterocarya fraxinifolia*) at home. This fast-growing, handsome tree can attain 100 ft in height, but is usually less, especially in cultivation. It forms a wide, spreading head supported by a short sturdy trunk, bearing deeply furrowed bark. The long, rich green, ash-like leaves have fifteen to twenty-seven oblong, lance-shaped leaflets. They act as a pleasing foil for the yellow-green, pendulous catkins that appear in summer. Later the tiny flowers give way to $1\frac{1}{2}$ ft long slender chains of small winged nutlets.

Above left: *Castanea sativa* in flower
Below left: *Juglans nigra*
Above right: *Carya ovata*
Below right: Young foliage and catkins of *Pterocarya fraxinifolia*

Magnolia and Tulip tree

Of all the trees that grow in the cooler temperate climes, the magnolia has the largest individual blossoms: Not all of the eighty known species are blessed with loveliness, but the best of them are superb, bearing chalice- or bowl-shaped flowers of a simple and appealing beauty. The genus *Magnolia* is of ancient lineage, the family to which it belongs being one of the first to evolve, millions of years ago. Among tree-sized species the Himalayan pink tulip tree (*M. campbellii*) is surely the most glorious. In its mountain homeland it can attain 150 ft, the sturdy twigs clad with bold, oval leaves up to almost 1 ft long. While the twigs are still bare in early spring, great flower buds balloon into growth and open

with the sun's warmth. At first they are chalice-shaped, but as they mature they take on the form of waterlilies, the finest being as much as 10 in across. In colour they vary from a beautiful rose-pink to pure white. Several named forms are known, including 'Darjeeling' which bears blooms of deepest pink.

Much smaller in all its parts is *M. kobus* from the mountains of Japan. Neatly pyramidal, at least until it reaches old age, the highest of the slender, ascending branches can reach about 30 ft. Before the leaves appear in early spring a profusion of starry white flowers garland the twigs in a very satisfying way. In its homeland it usually grows not too far from the rich dark evergreen columns of Japanese

cedar, which sets off the flame-shaped pillars of white to the very best advantage. Closely related and also Japanese is the willow-leaved magnolia (*M. salicifolia*), but whereas *M. kobus* has broad oval leaves, this has lance-shaped ones. The tree, also, is a little smaller and more slender and flowers at an earlier age.

In many eyes, the most beautiful of the Japanese magnolias is the yulan (*M. denudata*). This is a much more sturdy tree, eventually attaining up to 40 ft, with a more or less rounded outline and branches with a fascinatingly crooked outline. Before the leaves, each twig tip produces an upstanding, goblet-shaped flower of purest white. A tree in full bloom viewed against a clear, spring blue sky

is indeed a magnificent sight.

Some of the magnolia species are evergreen and one of the more impressive of the Asiatic species is *M. delavayi*. When mature this develops into a rather gnarled, spreading tree up to 40 ft or so, with leathery textured and massive leaves that are often more than 1 ft long. Although of rather sombre tones, each leaf is a matt finished sea-green above and rather bluish white beneath. In summer and at intervals into the autumn, beige tinted white flowers open. They are cup-shaped and spicily fragrant, but rather fleeting.

One must travel to the south-eastern states of the USA to see the finest of the evergreen magnolias at home. This is the bull bay or southern magnolia (*M. grandiflora*). Were it never to bloom, the deep and lustrous elliptic leaves, up to 8 in long and which densely clothe the sturdy branches, would be satisfying enough. But the best is yet to come. From summer through to autumn, huge waxy-petalled, cream waterlilies, sometimes as much as 10 in across, tip the erect, robust twigs in sequence. Heavily, and spicily fragrant they provide a magnificent accent to the dark glossy foliage. Staying in the south-eastern USA, but moving up to the mountain lime-stone valleys of North Carolina and parts of adjacent states, we find the largest leaved magnolia known to science. Known as the large-leaved cucumber tree and great-leaved magnolia (*M. macrophylla*) this 40–60 ft tall tree bears leaves that can attain 3 ft long and 1 ft wide. Roughly oval in outline they have two small rounded lobes at the base. Equally massive are the bowl to bell-shaped flowers of creamy-white and maroon which range from 8–12 in in diameter.

The saddle-shaped leaves of the tulip tree (*Liriodendron tulipifera*) are unique among the deciduous temperate trees. Up to 6 in long and wide, each leaf has four wide lobes and a truncated, usually shallowly notched tip. When folded down the midrib, the result really does look like a saddle. As the common name suggests, the flowers are tulip-shaped, but the colouring is much more subtle than that of any tulip. The ground colour is pale green, shaded bluish at the base and lit up within by orange markings. In due course, narrow, cone-shaped fruit develop. Also known as white wood, tulip poplar and yellow poplar in its native, eastern USA, the tulip tree is a stately species capable of attaining 100 ft with ease and exceptionally to 190 ft. It is particularly attractive in the autumn when the leaves turn bright, rich yellow. The straight grained timber is used for boat-building, furniture, boxes and pulp.

Far left: Flowers of *Magnolia campbellii*
Below: Flowers and foliage of *Liriodendron tulipifera*
Above right: *Magnolia salicifolia* in flower
Below right: *Liriodendron tulipifera* in winter

Edible Fruits

Apples, pears, plums and cherries are thought of as fruit trees and not as objects of arborescent beauty. But anyone who has seen orchards at blossom time will know what an impact on the scenery they can have. Indeed, several of the original species from which the modern fruits evolved and hybrids between them are much sought after by gardeners to beautify the landscape. Callery's pear (*Pyrus calleryana*) from China is a case in point. This is a medium-sized, somewhat thorny tree with broadly oval, richly glossy leaves and a massed display of a foamy white flowers in spring. The tiny pears that follow are scarcely edible, being like large brown peas. A selected form known as 'Bradford' is much planted in the

fragrance for yards around on warm days. The tiny, green apples that follow are astringent and virtually inedible. From the province of Hupeh in China comes a tree of similar appeal-but with rather stiffly ascending branches. This is *M. hupehensis*, a tree which the Chinese use as a tea substitute as well as appreciating the beauty of its pink and white blossom.

The wild crab apple of Europe and south-western Asia (*M. sylvestris*) is the progenitor of the domestic orchard fruit. It has smaller, smoother, almost glossy leaves and a profusion of small white, pink suffused flowers. Many forms have arisen which are noteworthy for for their brightly coloured crab apples in

shades of yellow, gold, crimson and orange. *Malus niedzwetzkyana* from south-western Siberia and Turkestan is very closely related but bears red-purple flowers and has the leaves flushed with red. It has given rise to several garden hybrids, the commonest being *M. x. purpurea* with bright, purple-red, flushed young foliage that fades to a duller shade later in the year.

The wild cherries have given us *Prunus avium*, colloqually known in Britain as gean or wild cherry and immortalized as the subject of A.E. Houseman's poem, *The Cherry*. Broadly pyramidal, at least until middle age, it is indeed a lovely tree when hung with multitudes of pendulous, long-stalked, snow-

USA and has the added advantage of crimson autumn foliage and no thorns.

The willow-leaved pear (*P. salicifolia*) can reach 40ft in height and is attractive for its narrow, grey, willow-like leaves and white flowers. Smaller but even more decorative is the selected form *P.s.* 'Pendula', a small weeping tree with very narrow, silvery foliage.

Many of the species and hybrids of wild or crab apple can give a superb floral display. Particularly noteworthy among the species is *Malus coronaria*, the common crab apple of eastern America. It forms a spreading tree to 30ft clad with warm grey bark and narrowly oval leaves. In May it becomes a cloud of shell-pink blossoms which cast their sweet

Left: *Pyrus salicifolia*
Above: Foliage and fruit of *Malus x* 'John Downie'
Right: Foliage and fruit of *Malus x purpurea*

white flowers. Well grown woodland trees can attain 80 ft but half this height is more usual. The bird cherry is even smaller and more slender in growth. Its main point of difference being the fluffy spikes of tiny flowers and very small cherries that follow. The wild black cherry or rum cherry (*P. serotina*) of the eastern USA is cast in a similar mould, but it is an imposing tree when well grown, being capable of reaching 90–100 ft, with a trunk diameter of up to 2 ft. The pendulous spikes of white flowers give way to pea-sized, lustrous black cherries which are used to flavour rum and brandy. The hard, close-grained, pinkish-brown wood is valued for the interior finish of houses, as it takes a fine polish and can be stained to imitate mahogany.

Among the wild forms of plum, the cherry plum (*Prunus cerasifera*) forms a decorative, rather round-headed tree to 30 ft or more. Its main season of charm is early spring when all the slender, previous years' stems break into a lather of pure white blossom. Later, small plums a little larger than a cherry change to shades of yellow or red. They are pleasantly edible and sometimes used to flavour brandy. This native of western Asia has long been cultivated in Europe, particularly Britain, where it is much used for hedging and as a root-stock for grafting domestic plums and peaches under the name of myrobalan plum.

There is also a purple leaved form with pale pinkish-purple flowers known as *P.c.* 'Pissardii'.

Juneberry and shadbush are vernacular names for various species of *Amelanchier*, native to North America. Although seldom cultivated for their edible fruits alone they do bear sweet, juicy berries which are regularly collected by townsman and countryman alike during their season. Amelanchier, like apple, pear, plum and cherry is a member of the rose family and closely related to the crab apple. Most of them are bushes, but the common Juneberry (*A. canadensis*) can occasionally reach 40 ft with a bole diameter of up to 16 in. Specimens

Left: Detail of flowers of *Prunus avium*
Above: *Prunus avium* in flower

of this size have grey bark furrowed into scaly ridges and attractively striped with sepia. In spring a profusion of white flowers foam over the twigs accompanied by tiny, neatly folded, white, hairy, young leaves. As the leaves expand, the white hairs gradually leave the upper surface to disclose a deep green lustrous surface. In autumn the green passes to shades of red and orange. The smooth-leaved shadbush (*A. laevis*) is a very similar tree, but the young leaves are hairless and look as if cut from bronze.

In Europe and particularly Britain yet another similar shadbush or Juneberry is found, sometimes erroneously under either of the previous names. This is correctly *A.*

lamarkii and may be distinguished by the young leaves being both hairy and coppery bronze.

Although not much eaten nowadays, the various species of mountain ash or rowan (*Sorbus*) provide a wide range of edible berries ranging through shades of red, orange, pink and white. They are mostly small elegant trees with ash-like foliage, though some species have oval leaves. The rowan (*Sorbus aucuparia*) grows throughout Europe and into western Siberia. It is the characteristic tree of the Scottish mountains and glens, where it was also often planted for its supposed magic properties to ward off witchcraft. Rarely exceeding 40 ft and usually much less, the

rowan is an erect tree with a light, ash-like leafage. Flattened heads of cream flowers are followed by clusters of red or orange berries that seem to drip from the twig tips and are a wonderful sight when viewed in the mellow golden light of an early autumn afternoon. *Sorbus discolor* is cast in a similar mould, but the red-stalked clusters of fruits are creamy yellow with a tinge of pink and the leaves colour red and orange in autumn. This description is based upon the tree one sees in gardens which may in fact be of hybrid origin. One needs to go to the hills of northern China to find again the true species.

Left: *Prunus cerasifera* in flower
Above: *Amelanchier lamarckii*

Also from China is *S. hupehensis*, a particularly decorative sort with foliage tinted blue-green and with white berries sometimes flushed pink. The mountain ash accolade must however really go to *S. sargentiana*. This robust species has sturdy, erect stems which bear large, sticky winter buds like those of the horse chestnut. These give way to sumptuous leaves a foot or so long and composed of seven to eleven slender-pointed leaflets. Massive heads of small, creamy flowers are followed by heavy clusters of scarlet fruits which ripen late and persist well into the winter. The supreme bonus is the autumn colour—a vivid crimson with an appealing matt finish.

The most popular of the sorbus species with undivided, oval leaves is the common whitebeam (*S. aria*), a tree of singular beauty when the leaves unfold in spring and early summer. To see it at its best one should visit its native hillside on a sunny and windy day. Then, the brilliant whiteness of the leaf undersurfaces continually shows, flashing in contrast with the richer green, upper surfaces. On the chalk and limestone soils of its European homeland a companion tree is often the sombre yew and the two set each other off in the most striking way.

Top left: Autumn foliage of *Sorbus sargentiana*
Centre left: Foliage and fruits of *Sorbus hupehensis* 'Rosea'
Bottom left: Young foliage of *Sorbus aria*
Right: *Sorbus aucuparia*

Trees with Pods

The trees in this section all have pod-like fruits in common. Most of them are members of the pea family (Leguminosae), which characteristically has the narrow, cylindrical or flattened fruits with a single row of seeds which are popularly known as pods. In addition, and somewhat to confuse the situation, some other plant families produce fruits that resemble pods. One example here is the indian bean (*Catalpa*), which belongs to the same family as jacaranda (Bignoniaceae).

The Judas tree (*Cercis siliquastrum*) is so-called because it is supposed to be the tree upon which Judas Iscariot hanged himself. There is nothing sombre or funereal about the tree itself however. Indeed, the reverse is true. In early spring just before the leaves expand, the twigs and larger branchlets become wreathed in clusters of bright rose-purple, pea-shaped flowers. Blooming continues as the distinctive rounded, notched-tipped leaves unfold. Later, red or purple tinted and greatly flattened pods develop. Unlike the pods of many plants, which split open suddenly and eject the seeds, these are whisked off by the strong winds of early autumn and being light and wing-like go sailing far and wide to new sites. This is more true of trees in their native southern and eastern Mediterranean regions where conditions are dry and warm. Several other kinds of Judas tree grow in North America and Asia. Those in the USA and adjacent Canada are better known as redbud owing to their prominent red flower buds on the bare twigs. The common redbud (*C. canadensis*) forms a small tree, rarely more than 25 ft tall, but occasionally in sheltered southern areas twice this. In spring it becomes smothered with crimson-purple blossoms of unexpected richness, which stains in a most effective way the stream and riverside habitats it favours. In its native south-western USA, the western redbud (*C. occidentalis*) can form a rugged tree up to 40 ft, but is usually less than half this size and rather shrub-like. A particularly large specimen can be seen at Indian Garden, an area of scrub and trees within the Grand Canyon just below the Grand Canyon Village. The reddish pods of the western redbud are particularly conspicuous and may

be seen in small windrows by track and roadsides after the first strong blow of autumn

The honey locust (*Gleditsia triacanthos*) has long been popular for its plumy foliage composed of several leaflets like those of a maidenhair. They are bright pale green in spring, mature to a bluish green and turn to yellow as they fade in autumn. The small greenish flowers are inconspicuous but are followed by striking, glossy, leathery-looking, maroon-brown pods a foot or more long. They are rather thick and contain a honey-tasting, green-yellow tissue. Often branching low down, the honey locust can attain a trunk diameter of 6 ft and rarely 100 ft high or more. A unique character of the bole and main branches is their armature of straight branching spines erupting from the rough grey-brown bark with its jagged sepia ridges. The spininess however is a variable character and some specimens never develop them. A native of the richer, moister soils of the eastern USA and Ontario, the honey locust has also been much planted elsewhere in North America and Europe. In recent years a form with bright yellow young leaves has arisen. Aptly named 'Sunburst', it has been widely planted in parks and gardens, lending elegance and colour to the scene.

Somewhat similar to the foregoing, but with smaller and less elegant leafage is the black locust or false acacia (*Robinia pseudo-acacia*). It has short, spiny twigs but no trunk spines and attractive clusters of white pea-flowers. These are fragrant and followed by slender, light brown pods 2–3 in long. This is another native of the eastern USA which has been much planted elsewhere and in Europe. In its homeland it is a valuable timber tree with a hard, greenish ochre-tinted wood that is very durable in contact with the soil. William Cobbett, the British political journalist and lover of the land and people of his birth, maintained that black locust wood was superior to English oak and wrote widely on its virtues. He also actively urged British landowners to plant this tree and turned his own garden into a nursery to fulfil the demand he created. He is said to have sold a million plants and thus is directly responsible for the widespread occurrence of robinia in Britain, most of the specimens seen being originals or descendants of those planted during the years immediately following 1823.

The Kentucky coffee tree (*Gymnocladus dioica*), like the honey locust, bears pods of massive dimensions, often 10 in long and $1\frac{1}{2}$ in wide. They are somewhat pulpy within and contain several large seeds, which were roasted and ground as a coffee substitute during the Civil War. The tree is tall, up to 100 ft, but usually less, with imposing foliage. Each leaf can be 2 ft or more long, composed of numerous oval leaflets. Although massive, the leafage casts but a light shade and makes a fine specimen tree for a large lawn. The Kentucky coffee is also appealing in winter,

when the stout, curiously crooked twigs, surfaced with a pale grey patina, etch the sky with bold scrawls.

China is the original homeland of the pagoda or scholar's tree, (*Sophora japonica*). It was, however, taken to Japan centuries ago and became extensively planted there. Later, European botanists visited Japan and thought it was a native, hence the species name. The pagoda tree is much akin to the black locust, but the leaflets are narrower and pointed and the white pea flowers are borne in larger clusters in late summer. Its main appeal is in the picturesque outline of the contorted branches that writhe outwards and become somewhat pendulous at the tips.

To find the next species of Sophora we must head for New Zealand. This is the kowai (*S. tetraptera*) and the national flower of that country. It forms a small tree, rarely above 35 ft but sometimes up to 45 ft. The slender leaves are made up of twelve to twenty-five pairs of neat, narrowly oval leaflets, the leafy branchlets so created being light and graceful. Rather tubular, pea-shaped, yellow flowers

Left: Flowers of *Cercis siliquastrum*
Above: Flowers of *Robinia pseudoacacia*
Below: Flowers and foliage of *Sophora japonica*

are borne in small pendent clusters, each blossom having a downswept standard petal and being $1\frac{1}{2}$–2 in long. A well flowered specimen is of striking appearance and it has become a popular ornamental where the winters are not too severe. Also known as kowai is the allied species *S. microphylla*. Its floral beauty is equal to that of *S. tetraptera* and the leafage marginally more decorative, being composed of narrow leaves split into twenty-five to forty pairs of tiny, oblong to rounded, dark green leaflets. Like many New Zealand trees and shrubs it passes through a very distinctive juvenile stage. After the germinating of the seed, a small bush develops formed of numerous, wiry, zigzag stems. After several years, a stronger stem arises in the middle which grows rapidly and becomes the main stem of the subsequent tree. Kowai pods are fascinating objects, resembling necklaces of winged beads.

Journeying across the Tasman Sea to Australia we find one of the most decorative of the wattles popularly called silver wattle (*Acacia dealbata*). The silvery powdered, fern-like leaves of this 40–50 ft tall tree are full of character and beauty and scarcely need the addition of flowers. Superlatives are inadequate to describe a silver wattle when draped in a fluffy cloud of spun gold flower balls. The individual flowers are minute, but several are aggregated into tiny pompons, which in turn are gathered into semi-pendent clusters in such profusion as to all but hide the leaves. The tree is much cultivated in the milder parts of the temperate regions and in southern Europe is grown extensively for the florists' trade, being exported as far north as Britain.

The cootamundra wattle (*A. baileyana*) is a somewhat similar species, but with even more beautiful silvery-blue foliage. It is however a much smaller tree, but quicker growing and shorter lived. Gracefully pyramidal when young it flowers with astonishing profusion and literally drips with pale gold flower balls. Although a native of a small area in New South Wales it has been much planted and is naturalized in many other parts of Australia. Variously known as the carob, locust and St. John's bread (*Ceratonia siliqua*) is an evergreen tree of dense, round-headed appearance, characteristic of the drier parts of the eastern Mediterranean region. The glossy, leathery leaves are divided into several pairs of broad, notched-tipped leaflets which in due season shelter clusters of tiny, greenish flowers. Sometimes the flowers actually erupt directly from the surface of quite large branches. They are followed by large almost woody pods with a sweet fibrous pulp and stone hard beans. The sweet unripe pods are used as cattle feed. Formerly they were an item of human food, particularly of the poorer peasants. It also seems likely that the locusts eaten by John the Baptist were the pods of this tree.

Spectacular and elegant are not overdone adjectives when applied to the various kinds of golden chain (*Laburnum*). Popular and much planted in the gardens of the cooler parts of the temperate zone they are still to be seen at their glorious best in the wild. To come upon a lone specimen gracing the edge of a woodland glade or clinging halfway up a grey limestone cliff is a sight to treasure. The common laburnum (*L. anagyroides*) forms a small tree rarely more than 25 ft tall. In spring it bears a profusion of pendent chains of golden pea flowers up to 7 in long with the young, silky, hairy foliage. Later, the leaves expand to a clover-like form, having three leaflets, hairy beneath and smooth above. Clusters of almost cylindrical pods follow the flowers. They are poisonous and should be kept out of the way of children.

The Alpine or Scotch laburnum (*L. alpinum*) grows larger, up to 35 ft or more with a sturdy smooth bole. The flower chains are longer, 1 ft or more, with wider spaced florets that have a light fragrance. The pods are flatter than those of the common laburnum and have the upper margin winged. The mating of these two species has given us the finest tree for garden decoration. Known as *L. x watereri* or *L. x vossii*, it more closely resembles the Scotch laburnum but has even longer chains of blossom arranged in denser formation. Being partially sterile it produces fewer and smaller pods, an advantage in the smaller suburban garden where children are about.

As already mentioned at the beginning of this section, not all trees with pods belong to the pea family. The Indian bean (*Catalpa bignonioides*) is an exception and bears large terminal clusters of foxglove-like blossoms above massive heart-shaped leaves. Individual flowers are white with a neatly crinkled finish and splashed yellow and red-purple at the mouth. They are followed by slender, pointed pods up to 16 in long. These hang on the tree long after the leaves have fallen and form a conspicuous feature. A native of the southeastern USA, the Indian bean forms a dome-headed tree of solid appearance and pleasing shape. Exceptional specimens can achieve 60 ft, but 30–40 ft is more usual.

Above left: *Sophora tetraptera*
Below left: Pods of *Catalpa bignonioides*
Above right: Young pods of *Ceratonia siliqua*
Above far right: *Acacia baileyana*
Right: *Laburnum x watereri*

Broadleaved Evergreens

In the temperate zone, particularly the cooler parts where so many trees stand leafless for half the year, evergreens greatly embellish and liven the winter scene, both in the wild and in our gardens. The common holly (*Ilex aquifolium*) is one of the most satisfying evergreens. Its glossy, spiny margined leaves are cheerful at all times of the year, especially in winter when garnished by the very familiar, lustrous red berries. In its native western Europe it can be seen in a variety of habitats, the commonest being as an understorey tree in deciduous woods of beech or oak. It can also be seen, usually in a more stunted or shrubby form, on open, grassy or rocky hillsides. Some of the finest specimens occur as hedgerow trees in Britain, where heights of 70 ft have been recorded and a bole girth of almost 6 ft. Mature trees are usually round-headed when well grown. Young trees on the other hand are narrowly pyramidal and elegant in outline. Although the leaves are thought of as wavy and spiny margined, shoots at the top of a tree and often all the leaves of an old tall specimen may be elliptical, bearing a single sharp terminal point. In spring the leaf axils bear small clusters of waxy, white fragrant flowers. Usually these are single sexed on each tree and male and female trees in fairly close proximity are needed to get a good crop of berries. Occasionally however hermaphrodite trees are found, easily recognized by regularly bearing fruits when isolated from their fellows.

Much planted in our gardens, the common holly has given rise to many variants, the most noteworthy having gold or silver variegated leaves, yellow or orange berries. The American holly (*I. opaca*) is similar in every way, but the leathery leaves are more of an olive green tint and much less glossy. It is native to the more sheltered parts of the eastern USA often on moist sandy soils near the coast.

The bay laurel, sweet bay and poet's laurel (*Laurus nobilis*) inhabits ravines and moist woods around the Mediterranean and is much planted elsewhere. Wreaths and crowns of its leaves were traditionally used to garland learned and famous men, particularly in classical times. Originally it was the tree of Apollo and was used as a symbol of victory. Baccalaureate and Poet Laureate are derived from the habit of poets and scholars wearing laurel wreaths when receiving academic honours. Young trees are conical in outline, broadening out as they age. The leaves are elliptic, rich green and sweetly aromatic. They are much prized in the kitchen and used to flavour fish and meat dishes of various kinds. Oil of bay is derived from the leaves. Fluffy clusters of yellowish flowers open in the leaf axils during spring and are followed by glossy black, ovoid fruits almost as big as a cherry.

The common strawberry tree (*Arbutus unedo*) also originates from the Mediterranean regions. It is not unlike a smallish leaved

Left: Hoar frost on leaves of *Ilex aquifolium*
Top right: Foliage of *Ilex opaca*
Centre right: Flowers and foliage of *Laurus nobilis*
Bottom right: Fruits of *Arbutus unedo*

laurel, but is quickly identified when bearing pendent clusters of urn-shaped, white waxy flowers or $\frac{3}{4}$ in wide, spherical, red fruits with a strawberry appearance. In late autumn, flowers and fruits may be seen together and if abundantly borne can present a striking appearance. Although edible, the fruits are insipid and barely palatable. Well grown specimens can reach 30 ft, but this is exceptional. The dense, rounded head is supported on a short, sturdy trunk covered in attractively shredding, dark red bark. Very similar, but having beautiful cinnamon-red bark is the hybrid *A. x andrachnoides*.

Noblest of the strawberry trees is the madrona (*A. menziesii*) from western North America. It can achieve massive proportions —70 ft tall and a bole girth of 28 ft. The branches are a startling red, clad with a thin, peeling bark. Older branches may take on a peachy tint, while the main trunk is often a dull deep purple. Young trees have an orange bark. Flowers and fruits are similar to those of *A. unedo* but orange-red and barely $\frac{1}{2}$ in across.

Above: *Rhododendron arboreum*
Below: Flowers of *Embothrium coccineum*
Right: Trunk of *Arbutus x andrachnoides*

In the Californian part of its home range, the madrona grows alongside such fine ornamentals as *Rhododendron occidentale*, the blue blossom (*Ceanothus thyrsiflorus*) and the mountain dogwood (*Cornus nuttallii*), all beneath the the shade of the coast redwood (*Sequoia sempervirens*).

Several of the evergreen rhododendrons attain tree size and can be among the most spectacular of all flowering trees. One of these is the aptly named *R. arboreum*, a native of Kashmir eastwards to Bhutan and also Ceylon. Picture a tree up to 40 ft in height, clad in narrow, rich green, glossy leaves bearing a layer of fawn to cinnamon felt beneath. Now cloak the branches with numerous trusses of narrowly tubular, scarlet bells, so that from a distance it appears as a pillar of fire. Imagine a group of these trees on a rugged mountainside with a backdrop of snow-clad Himalayan peaks—a sight never to be forgotten. It was one of the first rhododendrons to be introduced into European gardens from the Himalayas and is the parent of many fine garden hybrids.

Temperate South America has produced some fine evergreen trees which combine floral beauty and handsome or pleasing foliage. The aptly named Chilean fire tree (*Embothrium coccineum*) is among the best known with its willow-like smooth leaves and frothy masses of intense orange-scarlet flowers. It grows its best in the temperate rain forests of southern Chile, where in some areas it forms almost pure forests and soars up to 80 ft or more. Such a forest in bloom does indeed look as though caught in an intense but heatless conflagration.

Winter's bark (*Drimys winteri*) somewhat resembles embothrium but is a smaller tree with larger, proportionately broader leaves that have a blue-white patina beneath. In contrast however, the flowers are cool ivory white and pleasantly scented. They are borne in clusters like those of the wild cherry, each blossom having several, narrow, wavy-margined petals and a boss of yellow stamens and green stigmas. An infusion of the smooth, pinkish-brown bark provides a tonic and stimulant, but is seldom used nowadays. Winter's bark grows in the mountains or cooler lowland areas of much of South America.

Also white, but of a purer tone, is *Eucryphia glutinosa*, surely the finest flowering tree of this colour that Chile can provide, A sizeable and often rugged tree in its homeland, this eucryphia is erect in growth with a dense foliage cover of lustrous, dark green leaves, each composed of three to five, oval, toothed leaflets. The flowers are usually freely borne and almost obscure the leaves. They are bowl-shaped and composed of four broad petals which protect the central boss of slender yellow stamens. In gardens it has mated with another Chilean species (*E. cordifolia*) which is taller and has entire leaves. The result is *E. x. nymansensis*, a superb, ornamental, woody plant that surpasses its parents in beauty. In the colder parts of the temperate zone these eucryphias may be only partially evergreen.

Left: *Drimys winteri*
Below: Flowers of *Eucryphia x nymansensis*

More Flowers and Coloured Leaves

This section is a pot-pourri of highly decorative trees that just have to be mentioned but do not otherwise fit into the categories dealt with on previous pages.

Sometimes the vernacular names that a tree acquires—or any other plant for that matter—are curiously inadequate even when reasonably apt. The dove tree, ghost tree, pocket handkerchief tree, all apply to *Davidia involucrata* a unique species from western and central China. These names refer to the pair of snowy, leaf-like bracts that enclose and protect the small spherical clusters of insignificant flowers. They are indeed rather like neat pocket handkerchiefs hanging down or like tiny ghosts. At a stretch of the imagination

they may be likened to small curiously shaped doves hanging by their beaks (or tails) from the twigs. And yet none of these really does justice to what Ernest Henry Wilson, the great plant collector who introduced it into British and American gardens, considered to be 'the most interesting and beautiful of all trees of the north-temperate flora'. First discovered by the French missionary l'Abbé Père Armand David in 1869 in the mountain woods of western China, it was introduced to the French nursery firm of Vilmorin in 1897. This French introduction resulted in one seedling which, in the light of further exploration and collecting, proved to be a distinct variety and was named *D. involucrata vilmoriniana*. In 1904

Wilson was sent to China primarily to collect seeds of davidia, for its fame had gone before it and many gardeners and nurserymen wanted to obtain such a fabulous sounding tree. Wilson found over a score of trees on a precipitous slope in a rocky declivity. They varied from 35 ft to 60 ft tall, the biggest with a girth of 6 ft. He admired the boldly veined and toothed, slender-pointed, heart-shaped leaves and then the fluttering ranks of paired, white, floral bracts, the largest ranging from 5–8 in long and 3–4 in wide. His self-appointed task was then to photograph a flowering branch— all high up among the foliage. The only way to do this was to climb up a brittle-branched *Tetracentron* tree right on the edge of the precipice and balance precariously on a 4 in thick limb with a large plate camera. One false move would have meant plummeting about 200 ft to the rocks below. Such were the hazards of the plant collector's life before the small, roll-film camera was invented.

In a more simple fashion, the floral charms of the mountain dogwood (*Cornus nuttallii*) are equally appealing. Like davidia the main attraction also lies in white bracts that surround small insignificant flowers. The dogwood however has four to seven broadly oval, petal-like bracts arranged like the petals of a dog rose. Borne in profusion and backed by elliptic, rich green leaves, a tree of 30–40 ft high and wide can present a really eye-catching sight. As its vernacular name suggests, the mountain dogwood inhabits mountain forests, often among the frond-like growths of conifers which provide an appealing contrast. It can be found in all the western states of the USA and into Idaho and British Columbia. In autumn it has a further term of glory when the leaves turn to bright shades of yellow and red.

Left: Flowers of *Davidia involucrata laeta*
Right: Flowers of *Cornus nuttallii*
Below: *Cornus florida* in flower

The flowering dogwood (*Cornus florida*) is closely related, but it is much less of a tree and is usually seen as a large shrub up to 15 ft. Occasionally and in favoured positions it can reach 30 ft or more. Apart from the difference in stature, the flowering dogwood has much narrower floral bracts than the mountain dogwood and they are often tinted with pink or purple. It flowers even more prolifically and in some parts of its eastern USA homeland garlands the roadsides in a spectacular way.

The foxglove tree is a most apt name for *Paulownia tomentosa*. In spring before the leaves expand, clusters of rich, blue-purple, foxglove-shaped flowers expand, terminating the robust ascending twigs. A well grown specimen of 50–70 ft or more can be a stunning sight, especially viewed in the mellow late afternoon sunshine. Named for no less a personage than Princess Anna Paulowna, daughter of Czar Paul I, this tree is a native of China and is much planted in Japan and parts of Europe. It is also grown in the USA and has even become naturalized in some of the southern states. Paulownia forms a round-headed tree with massive heart-shaped leaves.

Above: Flowers of *Paulownia tomentosa*
Left: Foliage and flowers of *Oxydendrum arboreum*

In autumn, even before the foliage falls, the clusters of flowers buds can be seen, each one clothed in a dense layer of velvety brown hair.

Although a native of China and Korea, the goldenrain tree or pride of India (*Koelreuteria paniculata*) has been much planted in temperate Asia and since the mid-eighteenth century in Europe and North America also. A pleasing tree throughout the growing season, it has three highlights of beauty. The backcloth is a wide head of spreading branches clad with elegant ash-like foliage. In late summer every twig becomes tipped with airy trusses of small, bright yellow flowers, creating an intense gold haze of blossom. These are followed by intriguing, inflated lantern-like fruits that pass from pale green through red to warm, pale brown. In autumn the leaves turn a cheerful yellow before they fall.

Achieving upwards of 60 ft, the sorrel-tree or sour-wood (*Oxydendrum arboreum*), is the tallest of the deciduous members of the heath and heather family. It grows in moist, rich, woodland soils in the south-eastern USA and forms a rather narrow tree with a straight central trunk and horizontal branches that tend to be pendulous at their ends. The foliage is acid to the taste, like that of sorrel, and narrowly oval to elliptic. It has a lustrous, deep green, upper surface and grey-blue patina beneath, turning crimson in autumn. In late summer and often into autumn as the leaves change colour, charming flattened sprays of

urn-shaped white bells appear, lighting up the foliage in a delightful way.

Whoever heard of a fuchsia as big as an oak tree with a rugged bole and stout spreading branches? It may sound unlikely but it does exist in New Zealand and is known as *Fuchsia excorticata*. True enough it quite often is little more than a large shrub or a small tree, but specimens between 35–40 ft are not rare and do have a certain oak-like quality, even though the bark is an attractive golden-brown shade and thin and peeling. The small, oval to lance-shaped and sparingly toothed leaves are somewhat glossy with silvered undersides. In southern New Zealand at least, it is fully deciduous, elsewhere some leaves stay on during the winter. As the young leaves flush in the spring, and often on bare wood, the typical, pendulous fuchsia flowers appear. Each one is about 1 in long and is composed of a bell-like calyx tube bearing four flared pointed sepals. It starts pale green and whitish, gradually turning red-purple. Black-purple berries follow.

In its native Japan and China, the katsura tree (*Cercidiphyllum japonicum*) can form majestic specimens up to 100 ft. Whatever the height, this is always a graceful tree having well proportioned and tapering limbs and slender twigs. In spring the unfurling rounded leaves are light red. Later they mature to a bright, almost sea-green above, with blue-white undersides. Their true moment of glory

comes in the autumn when they magically turn to a clear, bright yellow, shot with tints of red, orange, pink and plum-purple. As the botanical name suggests, katsura has leaves like those of the Judas tree (*Cercis*). It is not in any way related however, being more nearly allied to the magnolias than to any other group.

Two of the finest autumn colouring trees are undoubtedly sweet gum (*Liquidambar styraciflua*) and the tupelo, black or sour gum (*Nyssa sylvatica*). Both favour moist soils, particularly by streams and riversides, and both are natives of the USA. Tupelo is found in the east from Maine south to Florida, while sweet gum is confined to the south-east, from Connecticut down to Cape Kennedy, Florida. The latter has glossy, elliptic leaves, the sweet gum has lobed, maple-like foliage. Under ideal conditions both can attain 100 ft, the sweet gum sometimes even more. In autumn they become pillars of riotous colour, crimson, scarlet, orange and yellow, lighting up the landscape in a spectacular way. Along with the maples, oaks, birches and poplars, they provide a splendid pageant for the dying year.

Left: The author admiring the trunk of *Fuchsia tomentosa*
Above: Autumn foliage of *Nyssa sylvatica*

Acknowledgments

The publishers are grateful to the following individuals and organizations for their kind permission to reproduce the pictures which appear on the pages shown:

A–Z Botanical Collection: 4, 14, 17 below right, 25 right, 39 left, 43 below, 49 below left, 50 above, 51, 55 above right, 57 above, 58–9, 70 above, 71 above, 74, 75 below, 76 right, 77 left, 77 right, 86 above, 92 above, 92 below.

Bernard Alfieri: 85 below.

Ardea: 50 below, 57 below, 75 above.

Douglas Baglin: 33, 62, 63, 66, 83 above right.

Barnaby's: 27 above, 38 above left, 78–9, 91 below.

Kenneth A. and Gillian Beckett: 11 below, 12, 16, 29 above, 31 above left, 31 below left, 32, 46, 53 above, 53 below, 93 left.

Biofotos: 13 above right, 13 below right, 19, 20, 30 left, 30 right, 35, 38 below, 38 right, 42 below, 47, 49 above, 54, 61 above, 61 below, 69 below, 71 below, 73 below left, 78 below, 83 above left, 84, 91 above, 93 right.

Bruce.Coleman: 1, 14–15, 56, 65, 80, 81 above, 85 above, 85 centre, 90.

Robert Estall: 28 above, 42 above.

Susan Griggs: (A. Woolfit) endpapers.

Robert Maiding: 2–3, 9, 17 above, 22–3, 34, 58 left, 64.

Peter Hunt: 29 below, 37 below.

N.H.P.A.: (H. R. Allen) 18, 7 below, 31 right, 43 above, 72, 76 left, 94. (K. A. & G. Beckett) 13 left, 81 below, 82 above, (S. Dalton) 28 below, 70 below, (E. K. Degginger) 36, 37 above, (G. E. Hyde) 41, 44–5, (A. Huxley) 17 below left, 22, 55 above left, 78 above, 78 centre, 82 below, 86 below, 88–9, 89, (A. Mitchell) 10, 73 above, 73 below right, (M. Savonius) 68, (J. Tallon) 21, 26, 55 below, 59, 60.

Photo resources: 24–5.

Picturepoint: 11 above, 39 right, 40, 48, 66–7, 69 above, 83 below, 86–7, back jacket.

Spectrum: Front jacket, 49 below right, 52

Line drawings: Barrington Barber

Index